Valerie Joyce
1610 Felton St.
San Diego, CA 92102

619-544-0925

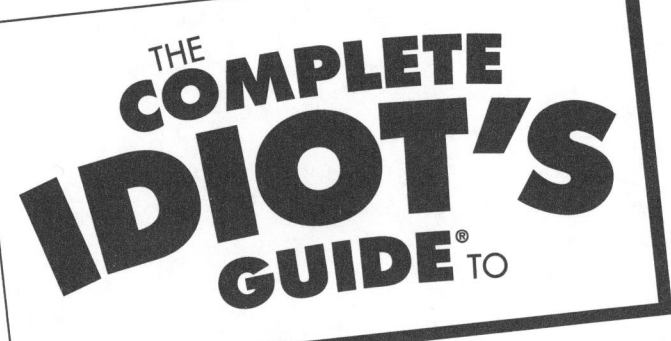

THE
COMPLETE
IDIOT'S
GUIDE® TO

Baby Sign Language

D1042961

Valerie Joyce
1610 Felton St.
San Diego, CA 92102

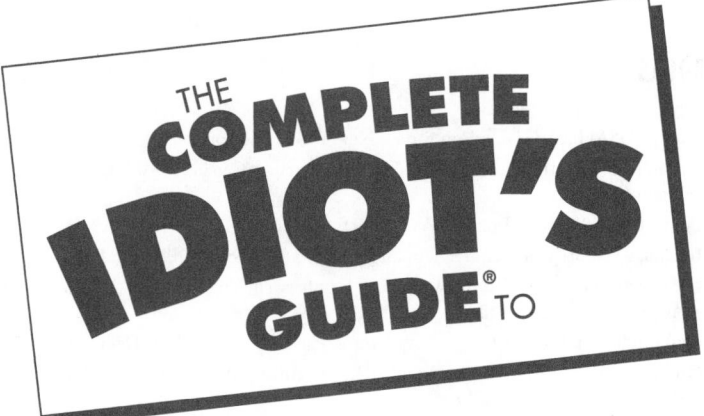

THE COMPLETE IDIOT'S GUIDE TO

Baby Sign Language

by Diane Ryan

ALPHA

A member of Penguin Group (USA) Inc.

ALPHA BOOKS

Published by the Penguin Group

Penguin Group (USA) Inc., 375 Hudson Street, New York, New York 10014, U.S.A.

Penguin Group (Canada), 10 Alcorn Avenue, Toronto, Ontario, Canada M4V 3B2 (a division of Pearson Penguin Canada Inc.)

Penguin Books Ltd., 80 Strand, London WC2R 0RL, England

Penguin Ireland, 25 St Stephen's Green, Dublin 2, Ireland (a division of Penguin Books Ltd.)

Penguin Group (Australia), 250 Camberwell Road, Camberwell, Victoria 3124, Australia (a division of Pearson Australia Group Pty. Ltd.)

Penguin Books India Pvt. Ltd., 11 Community Centre, Panchsheel Park, New Delhi—110 017, India

Penguin Group (NZ), cnr Airborne and Rosedale Roads, Albany, Auckland 1310, New Zealand (a division of Pearson New Zealand Ltd.)

Penguin Books (South Africa) (Pty.) Ltd., 24 Sturdee Avenue, Rosebank, Johannesburg 2196, South Africa

Penguin Books Ltd., Registered Offices: 80 Strand, London WC2R 0RL, England

Copyright © 2006 by Diane Ryan

All rights reserved. No part of this book shall be reproduced, stored in a retrieval system, or transmitted by any means, electronic, mechanical, photocopying, recording, or otherwise, without written permission from the publisher. No patent liability is assumed with respect to the use of the information contained herein. Although every precaution has been taken in the preparation of this book, the publisher and author assume no responsibility for errors or omissions. Neither is any liability assumed for damages resulting from the use of information contained herein. For information, address Alpha Books, 800 East 96th Street, Indianapolis, IN 46240.

THE COMPLETE IDIOT'S GUIDE TO and Design are registered trademarks of Penguin Group (USA) Inc.

International Standard Book Number: 1-59257-469-6
Library of Congress Catalog Card Number: 2005937197

08   07   8   7   6   5

Interpretation of the printing code: The rightmost number of the first series of numbers is the year of the book's printing; the rightmost number of the second series of numbers is the number of the book's printing. For example, a printing code of 06-1 shows that the first printing occurred in 2006.

Printed in the United States of America

Note: This publication contains the opinions and ideas of its author. It is intended to provide helpful and informative material on the subject matter covered. It is sold with the understanding that the author and publisher are not engaged in rendering professional services in the book. If the reader requires personal assistance or advice, a competent professional should be consulted.

The author and publisher specifically disclaim any responsibility for any liability, loss, or risk, personal or otherwise, which is incurred as a consequence, directly or indirectly, of the use and application of any of the contents of this book.

Most Alpha books are available at special quantity discounts for bulk purchases for sales promotions, premiums, fund-raising, or educational use. Special books, or book excerpts, can also be created to fit specific needs.

For details, write: Special Markets, Alpha Books, 375 Hudson Street, New York, NY 10014.

Publisher: *Marie Butler-Knight*
Editorial Director/Acquiring Editor: *Mike Sanders*
Senior Managing Editor: *Jennifer Bowles*
Development Editor: *Lynn Northrup*
Senior Production Editor: *Billy Fields*
Copy Editor: *Emily Bell*

Illustrator: *Carolyn Barcomb*
Cover Designer: *Bill Thomas*
Book Designer/Layout: *Becky Harmon*
Indexer: *Tonya Heard*
Proofreading: *Mary Hunt*

Contents at a Glance

Appendixes

Contents

Appendixes

Introduction

Once upon a not-so-long-ago time, a book that taught you how to communicate with babies before they could speak would be found in the Occult or Science Fiction section of the bookstore. But now that the subject has gone mainstream, here it sits next to all the other books on ways to be a better parent.

Actually, the word *mainstream* doesn't quite cut it. It's far too tame. Signing with hearing babies has become a national phenomenon! It's on the news, in magazines, and even in the movies. "It's something you can't afford *not* to do," your friends tell you. "But then your baby won't talk!" says your mother-in-law. Who's a parent to believe?

The questions are swirling around in your head. Is signing with a hearing baby really a good idea? Yes, say the experts. But not that long ago, some Chinese guru thought that binding a baby's feet was inspired. And what about the practical issues? Do you have time to do this? Will you have to learn a complete sign language when you had trouble with pig Latin in grade school? And what happens if you start signing and then decide to stop? Will your baby stutter? Or what if he gets *too good* at it and your mother-in-law is right? Maybe he won't speak at all!

Lots to think about, huh? If you're like most parents, you've already been online looking for more information. What did you find? Too many opinions and too many products, plus scads of stuff about creating smarter babies. Is baby sign language part of that, too?

That's another thing. When did we all get so competitive? Can't we just relax and enjoy our babies? Do we have to send in his application to Harvard before he's out of diapers? What if he'd prefer Yale? This is just too much for a parent to take! Can't anyone help?

That's where I come in.

Okay, so who am I and what can I offer? Allow me to answer the second question first: illumination, perspective, education, and guidance.

Now for the introduction: my name is Diane Ryan and I'm someone who has asked the very same questions that you're asking right now. But since I'm also a speech and language pathologist, my skepticism and concerns motivated me to dig deeper. So I studied the research, read the reports, reviewed the programs, talked to parents, tested what worked and what didn't, and created a program of my own.

Since I founded KinderSigns five years ago, I've personally taught hundreds of parents to teach their hearing babies to sign, both here in the United States and in Europe. Thousands more have learned through my online programs. Plus I've created an international network of instructors who now teach the KinderSigns technique in their own communities worldwide. So when it comes to finding an expert on the subject of teaching your hearing baby to sign, you don't have to look any further.

When Alpha Books contacted me to write a book on the subject, I asked myself, "Does the world need another book on how to teach sign language to babies?" Since you're reading this, you already know how I responded. While there may be other books, tapes, and DVDs on the topic, there is no *definitive* resource. One that looks at the research, the benefits, and the programs, and tells it like it really is.

My goal in writing this book is to dispel the myths, validate the truths, discuss the programs, convince you to sign with your baby—and then teach you how. You know those friends of yours who told you that signing with your hearing baby is something you can't afford *not* to do? Well, they were absolutely right.

Please note: throughout this book (for the sake of simplicity and my sanity), I have used the pronouns *he* or *him* when referring to babies rather than the awkward *he/she* combination. This deference to the masculine gender in no way reflects any bias or negativity toward baby girls. In fact, I had two of my own. (Hi, Michelle and Kristin!)

How to Use This Book

The book is divided into four parts:

Part 1, "Baby Sign Language Basics," separates facts from fiction and offers a solid foundation for your learning experience. You'll meet the researchers, study the benefits, and learn why teaching your baby to sign is a priceless gift to give your child.

Part 2, "Ready, Set, Sign!," provides everything you need to know to get started. You'll learn what signs to teach your baby and exactly how to teach him. Plus you'll discover that teaching your baby to sign is much easier than you thought.

Part 3, "The Transition to Speech," deals with what happens when the spoken word enters the picture. You'll learn how to increase your baby's sign language vocabulary while promoting his verbal language skills.

Part 4, "The Advanced Signer," is for those who want to continue signing into the toddler stage and beyond. You'll discover tips, techniques, and benefits unique to this special age group.

In addition, you'll find the following:

- **Baby Sign Language Dictionary.** Here you'll find more than 120 of the most popular signs to teach your baby. Each illustration clearly demonstrates how to make the sign and comes complete with written instructions to make the job even easier. The dictionary is divided into categories to help you decide which signs you want to teach your baby or toddler. I'm certain that you'll come to appreciate this valuable resource at every stage of your signing adventure.

- **Appendix A.** Have a question? There's a good chance that someone has already asked it. I'll answer the most popular questions here.

- **Appendix B.** Signing with your baby has to be fun. This appendix offers suggestions on how to reinforce the signs that you teach and have a great time while you're at it. Plus you'll find valuable suggestions on other ways to stimulate your baby's brain.

♦ **Appendix C.** While this book is all you need to teach your baby to sign, you'll find other helpful resources in this appendix, including baby sign language forums, informational websites, and other publications to enhance your learning and teaching experience.

♦ **Appendix D.** Keep track of your baby's signing progress by entering the date that you introduce a sign and the date your baby learns it. Clip out the journal and keep it handy to update babysitters and caregivers on your baby's progress.

Extras

Throughout this book, you'll also find sidebars that offer tips, cautions, and other tidbits of information:

Smart Signs

Check these boxes for tips and tidbits to make things go more smoothly and guarantee signing success.

Take Note

Here you'll find words of caution about how to avoid roadblocks and stay on track.

Behind the Signs

Check these boxes for interesting facts on the subject of babies and sign language. Great material for your next cocktail party!

Acknowledgments

Completing a project like this wasn't as easy as I thought it would be. In fact, it wouldn't have happened at all if it were not for the efforts of a special few: the editors of Alpha Books, especially Lynn Northrup, who honed my copy and made it better. Carolyn Barcomb, artist extraordinaire, who added warmth and personality to the illustrations. Steve Remington, my consultant and sage business manager. Michelle Rowley and Kristin Hanratty, my smart and successful daughters, for their encouragement and support. And most especially, to my husband Bob. No words can express my gratitude for who you are, what you have done and continue to do for me each and every day of my life.

Trademarks

All terms mentioned in this book that are known to be or are suspected of being trademarks or service marks have been appropriately capitalized, including, KinderSigns™, *Sign with Your Baby*™, and *Baby Signs*™. Alpha Books and Penguin Group (USA) Inc. cannot attest to the accuracy of this information. Use of a term in this book should not be regarded as affecting the validity of any trademark or service mark.

Part 1

Baby Sign Language Basics

Just when you thought that raising your hand to a child was a possible felony, along comes a school of thought that not only tells you that you *should*—but that your child will be much better off if you do. Tough love? No. Baby sign language.

You've heard about it, read about it, seen it on TV or maybe in the movies. It is, after all, an intriguing idea. Imagine, communicating with a baby before that baby can actually speak!

"Ridiculous!" your great-grandmother would have said. "Not a good idea," according to your mother-in-law. "Worth the effort?" you're asking yourself.

In Part 1, I'll answer the questions and address the concerns. The big one, of course, is why would anyone want to teach sign language to a *hearing* child? Can it, in fact, impede a baby's normal development?

Some of the answers will surprise you; others may intrigue you. Together, I hope they will motivate you to learn more about an innovative way to communicate with your baby—through sign language.

Chapter 1

What's All the Fuss About?

In This Chapter

- Discover what baby sign language is—and what it isn't
- Learn what it will and won't do
- Understand how hearing babies benefit from learning sign language
- Meet the people behind the signs and the science
- Make the decision: to sign or not to sign?

Congratulations! You are an open-minded parent, a person who hears about something unusual and wants to know more. Maybe you heard about signing with babies at your cousin Shelly's baby shower. But as you soon discovered, showers aren't ideal settings for in-depth discussions. Everyone's real focus is on those fabulous games and dahhh–ling baby gifts.

Or maybe TV news was your source. There was a whopping 60 seconds devoted to the concept one night. Remember, it was right after the Washington scandal and before the Wall Street report? Interesting information, to be sure. But are you going to make a decision as important as this based on an info-minute?

So, hats off to you! You've done the responsible thing and are investigating the idea first-hand. You'll make an excellent parent, if you haven't already achieved that status.

I assume you're ready, then? Highlighter uncapped? You're about to learn all there is to know about teaching a hearing baby to sign.

Exactly What Is Baby Sign Language?

Simply put, baby sign language is a way to communicate with your baby before your baby can speak by teaching him a few basic gestures or signs. It's a way to bridge the gap between his gurgling stages to the time when he can actually talk. Some parents continue well beyond that stage. That's optional.

In fact, there are a number of options available to you when it comes to signing. One has to do with why you want to do it in the first place. If you're like most parents, you're considering it as an interim method of communication before your baby's first words. Other parents think of it as a way to begin a lifelong skill. There's one thing everyone needs to agree upon, however. In order to be successful, it has to be fun for all involved.

Now let's talk about what baby sign language *isn't*. It is not, in my opinion, part of "Super Baby" mania, the current craze to create smarter, higher-thinking infants and children. And while you may find baby sign language books, tapes, and DVDs in the same aisle as the IQ-boosters, they're not the same thing.

Do those baby development products work? They very well may, but that's not my area of expertise. What I *do* know is that teaching a baby to sign builds on his natural tendency to gesture. It *enhances communication*, *builds stronger connections in families*, and *reduces a pre-verbal baby's frustration* when he can't get his point across. Those are the *primary* reasons that you should sign with your baby. It will help you get closer to him and form a tighter bond. Plus your baby will really love the experience! If there are cerebral fringe benefits beyond that—*and there are*—all the better.

A Simple and Natural Way to Communicate

Teaching a baby to sign is simple. It's about as far from rocket-science as you can get. Yes, it does involve some patience and dedication, but there's a huge payoff at the end of the day and it's well worth your investment. At the very least, it's something you should seriously consider.

When you teach your baby to sign, you will use signs that are part of American Sign Language (ASL), the official language of the deaf community in the United States. While some signs have been adapted to make them easier for a baby to make, the majority are the genuine articles. That explains why many parents consider this as the first step in introducing a second language to their child.

Oh, I'm *so* sorry! To the lady who's hyperventilating in Houston, let me clarify that last statement. Yes, you will be using authentic ASL signs, but you *don't* have to learn an entire sign language! You'll start with a few basic signs and can add as many as you like from there. Feel better?

Here's another plus. Signing with your baby is natural and instinctive. Depending on your baby's age, he may already *be* signing, in fact. Babies raise their hands to be picked up. They point to things they want. And think how easy it is to teach a baby to wave "bye-bye." That means that when you teach your baby to sign, you are simply taking advantage of what comes naturally.

Is it essential that you teach your baby to sign? No. Will your baby suffer if you don't? Well, maybe *suffer* isn't the right word, but he (and you) will miss out on a closer connection, plus a host of other astonishing benefits if you pass it up.

Behind the Signs

Interest in baby sign language soared after it was featured in the 2005 movie, *Meet the Fockers*. In the film, Robert DeNiro's "grandson" stole the scene by signing that he was hungry, sleepy, and would probably need a diaper change. The role was actually played by baby-signing twins whose mother had taught them to sign.

Think of this as a golden opportunity. Actually, it's much more valuable than gold. It's a priceless opportunity to find out what your baby is thinking. It's a way to look into his world through *his* eyes. Why just guess at what your baby wants or needs? If you teach him to sign, he can tell you himself.

When you teach your baby to sign you don't have to wait until he's ready to communicate with words. That could be months away. Think of all the time you may be wasting! (Especially when you factor in the teenage years when he probably won't speak to you at all.) So give your baby the tools he needs to communicate and start a two-way dialog—*right now.*

Why Teach Sign Language to a Hearing Baby?

It used to be that sign language was associated only with the deaf culture. No one saw the benefits of teaching sign language to hearing children. After all, what was the purpose? They would speak eventually. And then someone came along who thought outside the box. That's how good ideas usually happen. In this case, it was an extraordinary one.

While working as an interpreter for the deaf in Alaska in the late 1970s, Joseph Garcia noticed that the hearing babies of deaf parents communicated at a much earlier age than children of hearing parents. That observation piqued his interest, sparked additional research, and resulted in a practical system to teach the technique to parents. We'll learn more about Garcia and his *Sign with Your Baby* program later. But for now we should credit Garcia with rephrasing the question that we started with. Instead of asking *why* anyone would want to teach sign language to hearing babies, Garcia asked, "Why not?"

Some might say, "I'll tell you why not. Don't I have enough to do? Plus I already know what my baby wants and needs. I can tell by the way he cries. His hunger cry is different from his cry for attention. And when he's in pain, I can tell that, too."

There is a lot of truth to that, of course. Mothers, especially, have a sixth sense when it comes to interpreting their baby's cries and body language. But a *signing* baby can share more *specific* information about what he wants or needs plus he'll scoop up a host of secondary benefits along the way.

Speaking of benefits, we'll delve into them (and the supporting research) more specifically later on in the book, but for now, let me tantalize you with this. Babies who sign …

- Are less frustrated.

- Have closer bonds with their parents and caregivers.

- Develop larger vocabularies.

- Become better readers.

- "Outsmart" babies who don't sign.

> **Take Note**
>
> While baby sign language has long-term intellectual and emotional advantages for your baby, your primary reason for signing should be to have a less frustrated, well-adjusted child. Plus it's fun!

The Biggest Misconception

Is there a downside to teaching your baby sign language? I know what you're thinking. It's the number one question I get. And the answer is a resounding NO! What you *really* want to know is, "If I teach my baby to sign, won't his speech be delayed?"

In fact, just the opposite is true. If you teach your baby a few simple signs, he'll speak *earlier*. And that's *sign-tifically* proven! (More on that later, too.) Now you can add *earlier speech* to the list of benefits I just mentioned.

Your question, by the way, is a good one. It's logical to think that by teaching your baby to sign you might be giving him a reason *not* to talk. But let's look down the road a bit further.

When you introduce a specific sign to your baby, you will *talk* to him at the same time. Rule #1 is that you must always *say* the word as you make the sign. You never sign without speaking.

> **Smart Signs**
>
> Don't listen to those who tell you that sign language will delay your baby's language development. Just the opposite is true. Signing babies speak earlier than those who don't. And that's a fact!

And there's this: Research tells us that parents of signing babies spend more time with them. Suddenly "babydom" takes on a new dimension. It becomes less custodial. Signing babies can actually *participate* in the family dynamic. The family spends more time with him playing, reading, labeling things, asking him questions, responding to those same questions, and talking and talking ... beginning to get the picture?

What Will Your Baby Be Able to Tell You?

Maybe this will help convey the idea. Let's visit the Humdrum household. They've never heard about baby sign language.

It's 2:30 A.M. and 12-month-old Amanda starts to cry. Mom gets up and goes to her room. She goes through the mental checklist. She feels Amanda's diaper. Totally dry. She offers her some water. Amanda cries even louder. She puts her lips to the baby's forehead. No fever. Now Amanda is screaming. And Mrs. H. is starting to panic.

Meet the Seinworthys. They live right down the street from the Humdrums and, you guessed it, they know all about baby sign language. In fact, they have been signing with little Bradley since he was seven months old. Let's take the same scenario and see how it applies to them.

It's 2:30 A.M. and 12-month-old Bradley starts to cry. Mom gets up and goes to his room. She goes through the mental checklist. She feels Bradley's diaper. Totally dry. She offers him some water. Bradley cries even louder. She puts her lips to the baby's forehead. No fever. Now Bradley is screaming.

Mrs. Seinworthy puts her two index fingers together in Bradley's sightline. It's the sign for "pain." Bradley makes the same sign in front of his mouth. Mom realizes that he's teething again. She gets his medicine and rubs it on his gums. A few minutes later, Bradley stops crying and falls back asleep. And Mrs. S. goes back to bed.

Pretty amazing, don't you think? A baby who can sign can tell you when he's in pain and also *where it hurts!* He can tell you when he's hungry, thirsty, and if he needs help. And get this, he can even tell you when he needs a diaper change! Truly extraordinary—especially when you consider that a baby can "tell" you all these things before he is able to utter a single word.

How Is All This Possible?

Research has shown that while babies lack the fine motor skills to speak, they do have the ability to understand and use language as early as six to seven months—if they are given the right tools and guidance. While speech may be more than six months away, a baby's receptive language skills significantly improve after only six months on the planet. So has his ability to manipulate objects with his hands. Why wait for your baby to speak his first words? He may be ready to communicate *now*!

Speaking of *speaking*, think about how really complicated the act of talking is, especially to a baby. To us, it's second nature. We have something to say and out it comes. But speech is an intricate and exacting dance.

Depending on the sounds or words you want to say, your tongue must be in a precise location, your lips need to coordinate with your teeth and you have to control your breathing to direct the flow of air, all the while making sure that you have enough left over so you don't pass out. Whew! A baby's brain needs about a year or more to even begin to take on that task!

Can All Babies Do This?

As you know, gesturing is a natural tendency for a baby. It's something that he'll do even if you don't follow through with this program. Babies are mimics. They take their lead from the people who surround them. They learn to speak by listening to you. And they'll learn to sign by watching you.

So whether or not a baby will sign has little to do with the baby. All babies can learn to sign. How fast they'll learn and how many signs they'll make are the things in question. But you already know the variable, right? The degree of signing success a baby achieves is in direct proportion to the level of dedication and enthusiasm of his parents!

By the way, I've taught baby sign language for five years in the United States and Europe and have never heard a parent say that their baby just couldn't grasp the concept. While there are obvious differences in every baby's ability, all babies can learn to sign.

Is This Appropriate for Deaf Babies, Too?

As I've mentioned, some parents have long-range intentions when they start teaching their baby sign language. But most parents will only sign until their baby's speech surpasses his signing ability. A deaf baby, obviously, has a much greater challenge than a hearing child. He needs a lifelong skill to be able to communicate. Whether a deaf baby is taught lip reading or sign language or a combination of both, he needs a more structured program specifically designed for that tiny individual and his particular level of hearing loss.

The techniques that are presented in this book are designed to *enhance* a baby's ability to communicate, not establish it. These demonstrations are based on the premise that the baby has the ability to hear and will eventually produce the sounds and words that are being presented to him. Will teaching these signs to a deaf baby hurt him? Of course not. But this program doesn't go far enough nor is it comprehensive enough to address a deaf baby's special needs.

Back to the Beginning

Maybe you're the type of person who doesn't care about the origin of things. To you, Darwin's no big deal. You live in the present and don't like to look back. If that sounds like you, skip this part. It isn't mandatory reading.

But if you're like I was at first, you may still be somewhat skeptical. You need more information—especially when your baby is involved.

Who are these people who cooked up this idea? What are their credentials? Do these so-called experts really have something important to say, or are they just trying to stretch their 15 minutes of fame to an hour?

So let's back up to the beginning and meet the baby sign language pioneers. At the very least, it's interesting reading. You may even be able to use some of it when there's a lull at your next cocktail party. And who knows? One day you might be a contestant on *Jeopardy* when the category pops up. ("I'll take Baby Sign Language Pioneers for $500, Alex.")

The Prime Mover

The interest in teaching sign language to hearing babies began in the late 1980s with two separate and significant research projects conducted by Joseph Garcia, a student at Alaska Pacific University, whom you met a few pages ago, and the team of Linda Acredolo and Susan Goodwyn, then Ph.D.'s at University of California, Davis. While their research was independent and distinct, the three had one thing in common. They used what they had around the house to formulate and test their theories: their kids.

As an undergraduate student, Joseph Garcia became fascinated with the idea of communicating through gestures or signs. While no one was deaf in his family, he thought that learning sign language would be interesting and he began to study it in earnest. Once he had a solid grasp of on American Sign Language (ASL), Garcia was certified as an interpreter for the deaf and became involved, both personally and professionally, with the deaf community. It resulted in an observation that changed his life—and the lives of many to come.

While spending time with deaf friends, Garcia noticed that the normal-hearing babies of deaf parents were able to communicate basic wants and needs at around 10 months of age. How was that possible? Simple. Their parents had taught them a few basic signs.

Behind the Signs

American Sign Language (ASL) is used in the United States and in English-speaking Canada. Many countries have their own sign language and some, like British Sign Language (BSL) have dialects. That means that someone in London signs differently than a guy wearing a kilt in Scotland.

Garcia contrasted this with the communicative ability of hearing babies with hearing parents. Around that age (10 months), they hardly communicated at all! Intrigued by this disparity, Garcia decided to make it the focus of his Master's thesis.

During his research, Garcia discovered that hearing children were able to produce simple signs at around eight months and some exceptional children as early as six months. Certainly this was far earlier than any baby could articulate any *spoken* word.

Garcia also found that once a signing child began to speak, he had a better grasp of grammar and language in general. Using his infant sons Stratton and Damien as "test subjects," Garcia validated his theories first-hand on the home front.

Behind the Signs

There is evidence that sign language benefited the hearing community before the sixteenth century. During that time Benedictine monks used sign language to communicate with one another when they observed long periods of silence.

Joseph Garcia's program evolved into the popular book/video program, *Sign with Your Baby: How to Communicate with Infants Before They Can Speak* (see Appendix C). Like this program, it's based on using American Sign Language as the basis for communicating with a baby through signing. For more information, visit www.sign2me.com.

The Lady Ph.D.'s

The findings of the Acredolo-Goodwyn team also stemmed from simple observations. In 1982 when her daughter Kate was a year old, psychology professor Linda Acredolo noticed that she was making an "itsy bitsy spider" with her hands whenever she saw one of the critters. When Kate spotted a flower, she would wiggle her nose as if sniffing it. Then there was a third event, one that's especially interesting.

It was time for Kate's 12-month check-up at the pediatrician's office. While they were in the waiting room, Kate was naturally attracted by the large aquarium there and toddled over for a better look. But then, according to Linda, she did something strange. She started to *blow*.

Dr. Mom was puzzled by the behavior and after the appointment, she took Kate home for a nap. As she put her down in her crib, Linda "activated" the mobile that hung over it. It was fashioned of brightly colored fish—and in order to make it rotate, Linda had to blow on it. Instantly, she became aware of the connection her daughter had made. Without any instruction, Kate was communicating with her own form of sign language.

As you might imagine the learned professor wanted to find out more. She had lots of questions:

♦ Do all children do this or just my daughter?

♦ Are there other signs or gestures that Kate might be using that I'm unaware of?

♦ Can I become an expert on this, create a national phenomenon appear on *Oprah* and make a fortune?

Smart Signs

Notice how simple observation is key to learning and discovery? Like Linda Acredolo, pay close attention to your own baby. See if he is making signs or gestures on his own. If he is, that's a sure sign that he's ready to learn others.

(Okay, I made up that last one—but that's just what happened.)

And so her quest began. Linda partnered with her colleague, Susan Goodwyn, now a professor of psychology and child development at California University, Stanislaus and an associate researcher at the University of California. Together they studied, observed, and questioned other parents. As scientists, they did things the right way. Backed by a federal grant, they compared babies who signed with babies who didn't. Then they followed and documented their progress. We'll look into those findings in greater detail in the next chapter.

Based on Acredolo and Goodwin's research, *Baby Signs: How to Talk with Your Baby Before Your Baby Can Talk* (see Appendix C) was published. The program promotes a short-term sign language experience and recommends a combination of baby-friendly American Sign Language (ASL) signs plus signs and gestures that parents and babies come up with on their own. For more information visit www.babysigns.com.

Take Note

There are many baby sign language books and tapes available that are based on the findings of the baby sign language pioneers. No matter which program you use remember that your final goal is not just to get your baby to sign—but to *speak*.

Why Listen to Me?

While the programs I've just discussed are excellent resources, you've purchased this book instead. Let me assure you that it's all you'll need. The baby sign language method you're about to learn is based on the KinderSigns approach. Since 2001, parents and childcare professionals in over 40 countries worldwide have used the KinderSigns method to teach babies sign language. Some parents have even "gone professional" and started their own business as KinderSigns instructors. (For more information, visit www.kindersigns.com.)

The method in this book is also the only program that uses authentic American Sign Language (ASL) *and* was developed by a speech and language pathologist. *(C'est moi.)* Of equal importance is the fact that this program places a far greater em-phasis on stimulating your baby's *verbal* language development than the others. And that's even more important than teaching your baby to sign.

The Least You Need to Know

- Baby sign language is a way to communicate with a hearing baby before the baby can speak.

- While there are many benefits, the primary reason to sign with a baby is to reduce the baby's frustration and to promote a closer parental bond.

- Joseph Garcia is largely credited with first discovering that babies can communicate before they can speak through sign language.

- The spontaneous signs her daughter made prompted Linda Acredolo, Ph.D. to partner with fellow Ph.D. Susan Goodwyn to conduct research into the baby sign language phenomenon.

- The method you will learn in this book is based on the KinderSigns program and utilizes American Sign Language (ASL).

- This form of sign language is not comprehensive enough to be used as a communication system for deaf babies.

Chapter 2

How Your Baby (and You) Will Benefit

In This Chapter

- ◆ Learn more about the researchers
- ◆ Marvel at their discoveries
- ◆ Learn the benefits of baby sign language
- ◆ Rid yourself of all doubt

Welcome to "Baby Sign Language University," the most cerebral part of the book. You met some of the "faculty" during orientation in the previous chapter. In case you were absent that day and no one took notes for you, we talked about how the idea of pre-verbal communication with babies got started. Like you, everyone was skeptical at first. All good scientists are. But they poked, postulated, and finally pronounced that teaching sign language to a hearing baby was a sound proposition—with benefits too amazing to pass up.

Now it's time to take a closer look at how our learned scholars arrived at their conclusions. Then we'll talk about how you and your baby will benefit from what they found. This is important information, class, so pay attention! You never know when there will be a pop quiz. That means you too, Mom.

A Cinematic Approach

In our last chapter, you were introduced to Linda Acredolo and Susan Goodwyn, both Ph.D.'s with a host of other impressive credentials. We talked about how Linda's daughter's spontaneous attempts at signing prompted two decades of research with her learned colleague. While there have been other studies in the field, their research has been the most publicized.

Since any research can be dry and hard to swallow, let me try to make it more palatable for you. If Hollywood were to take this material and make it into a major blockbuster, they would first need financial backing. So did Acredolo and Goodwyn. In 1989, they headed for the National Institute of Health and managed to convince potential backers that studying the long-term effects of teaching hearing babies sign language was worthy of a grant. Their earlier research had convinced the dynamic duo of the short-term benefits. Now they needed to know more.

The Premise:

It was a simple one, really, presented in the form of a question. What were the advantages (or disadvantages) to teaching sign language to hearing babies?

The Players:

Over 140 families with 11-month-old babies were cast. Each family had to fit a certain criteria to make sure that they were all at a similar stage of development. Family income and education were considered as well as each baby's sex, birth order, and ability to vocalize.

The Plot:

One third of the families were shown how to use sign language. Another third were encouraged to speak to their babies more often than they would normally. The remaining families were the control group.

They were told to simply do what comes naturally, to continue caring for their babies as they would normally. None of the groups was aware of the other participants and no one had any idea what the whole thing was about.

The Contract:

Each family agreed to spend two years under the microscope. If this were TV, it would be like a reality show without the cameras. Their progress would be monitored and after 24 months, the signing babies would be tested to see if there were any benefits or negative side effects. Then comparisons would be made with the other groups.

> **Take Note**
>
> Keep in mind that the results that are mentioned in these studies are based on the "average" and will not be the same for each child. That means that your baby may not reach these lofty heights. He could soar even higher!

The Exciting Conclusion:

- At 24 months, the signing babies had the vocabularies of 27- or 28-month-olds.

- At 24 months, they used significantly longer sentences.

- At 36 months, the signers spoke like 47-month-olds. Almost a full year ahead!

Bottom line? The signing babies outperformed and outclassed all other groups in the study.

The Sequel:

Pretty impressive, don't you think? But the learned ladies didn't stop there. Scientists always want to know more. In this case it was whether or not there would be any *long-term* effects to teaching a hearing baby to sign. So what did they do? They waited eight years and paid those same families another visit.

The children, now age eight, were tested to see what happened after all that time. Were there any long-term benefits? Were there any "bad seeds" in the bunch?

The Reviews:

Two thumbs up. Way up! The reviews were all positive. In general, when tested eight years later, babies who had learned some basic sign language had better language and cognitive skills than those who hadn't.

Smart Signs

Your IQ is determined by multiplying your mental age by 100 and then dividing it by your chronological age. For example, if your two year old has the intellectual level of a three year old, his IQ is 150. One smart kid! (By the way, IQ is an indication of your *ability to learn*, not how smart you are.)

◆ Signing babies had an average IQ of 114 compared with 102 for their non-signing counterparts.

◆ Signing babies demonstrated an above-average understanding of English plus their grammar and syntax were more advanced.

Added Star Power

While Acredolo and Goodwyn are the best-known "celebrities" in the field, having promoted their findings on the talk show circuit, there's another star on the Walk of Fame that can't be ignored.

Marilyn Daniels (Maltese), Ph.D., now professor of Communication Arts and Sciences at Penn State University, is probably the most prolific researcher on the subject of children and sign language that we have today. While she acknowledged the Acredolo-Goodwyn studies, she decided to dig deeper into the correlation between sign language and intellectual and academic development.

Dr. Daniels' research stemmed from an observation her graduate students made. They wondered why the hearing children of deaf parents seemed to do so well in reading and writing. Logical thinking told them that since these children lived in a language-deprived environment, they should be struggling in these areas, not excelling in them.

And so, Dr. Daniels did what any self-respecting academician would do. She designed a study! Numerous studies, in fact. The results of her research were first presented in 1994:

◆ Signing children have better recognition of letters and sounds. They are better spellers and have larger vocabularies.

♦ Children who sign speak better and have more advanced communication skills than nonsigners.

♦ Children who had been taught American Sign Language had higher reading levels than those who had no ASL instruction.

The results of Dr. Daniels' work have been published in her book, *Dancing with Words: Signing for Hearing Children's Literacy* (see Appendix C). In addition to encouraging parents to sign with babies and children, she recommends that teachers incorporate American Sign Language (ASL) into their everyday curriculum. Educators who have followed her advice give the idea "rave reviews" and claim that children not only enjoy the experience but that sign language actually does accelerate literacy and learning.

Behind the Signs

Want another way to boost your baby's IQ? There is solid evidence that children develop higher intellectual ability if they receive love and a proper diet as babies, particularly if they're breastfed.

Exactly How *Your* Baby Will Benefit

Now you know why teaching your baby to sign is so important. Basically, it's a way to give him a head start in life. But the researchers forgot to mention that signing with your baby is also lots of fun! And, as you are about to see, that's only one of the side dishes that's served with the main course.

Let me get back to the researchers for a minute. Didn't you find it a bit bothersome how truly impersonal those scientists could be? It was all about babies as "statistics" and babies as "test subjects." Well, it's a good thing that I take a more caring approach. What about *your* baby? How will *he* benefit from the experience? Okay, get ready. This time it's personal.

Take Note

I've mentioned this before, but it bears repeating. The benefits that are mentioned in this section are based on the "average." Your baby may not do as well, or he may outperform them all.

Emotional Benefits

There are countless gifts you can give your baby. But signing parents give their little ones something that not even Bill and Melinda Gates can buy—emotional well-being.

◆ **Less frustration.** When you give your baby a way to express his feelings, there is little or no reason for him to be frustrated. He'll discover that signing empowers him and that it's more productive than crying, whining, or throwing a fit. He now has the tools to communicate specific information to you.

◆ **Greater self-esteem and self-confidence.** Studies show that reaching out and being understood by a grown-up is important for any child. A signing baby grows up thinking well of himself because of the positive responses of everyone around him. Sure beats an inferiority complex.

◆ **A closer parent-infant bond.** When you sign with your baby you'll spend more time together. And we're talking "quality time" that's chock-full of positive interactions. You'll find that parenting is less custodial and reactive. And your baby will discover much sooner who's boss. (Guess who *that* might be?)

Social Benefits

Once your baby has an effective way to communicate, he'll play a more active role in the family dynamic and develop a closer bond with siblings and caregivers. He'll be able to make demands and get away with it. Everyone will think it's *soooo* cute! Then there's big bro and sis. They'll feel like VIPs teaching the little one new signs. And when the babysitter takes over, she'll be able to speak the baby's language and he can boss her around, too!

> **Behind the Signs**
>
> Signing babies can initiate "conversations." They can "tell" you that they saw a dog or an airplane and want you to pay attention to it. Parents say that they never realized how many airplanes flew overhead until they taught their babies that specific sign.

Language Benefits

When you sign with your baby, you spark his language ability, not dampen it. A baby's first sign stimulates his interest in two-way communication and motivates him to perfect his skills all the way to the spoken word.

- **Early communication.** Your baby has the ability to understand what you're saying long before his muscles enable him to respond. Once sign language bridges that gap, he won't have to wait to let you know that you're not living up to his expectations. He can start critiquing you—right now!

- **Earlier speech.** If you're worried that sign language will delay your baby's verbal language development, forget it. Just the opposite is true. You read the research and if you didn't, here's a re-cap. Sign language actually *helps* babies learn to talk. Babies who sign speak *earlier* than those who don't. And that's a fact.

- **Larger vocabulary.** By the time a signing baby reaches the toddler stage, he has about 50 more spoken words than a non-signing tyke. At three, he'll speak and understand at a four-year level. But since we all know that *your* child's not average, who knows what and how much he'll be saying!

> **Take Note**
>
> It is a proven fact that babies who sign speak *earlier* than those who don't. That means that signing will *not* stifle your baby's verbal language development. Do not listen to anyone who tells you differently. In this care, even ignore your own intuition. You have enough to worry about. Now you can cross that off your list.

Cognitive Benefits

When you sign with your baby, you get a child who speaks earlier and is more emotionally secure … and who is smarter than the kids who don't sign!

- **Greater brain function.** Research on the brain has uncovered some amazing facts. Here's one of them: Spoken language is stored in the left side of the brain. Information obtained visually is stored in the right side. Since signing involves spoken language *and* eye involvement, both hemispheres of the brain are used. Simply put, signing will help build more of your baby's brain and greater brain function.

◆ **Higher IQ.** Of course nothing can be 100 percent guaranteed, but research indicates that babies who sign have higher IQs than babies who don't. Researchers Acredolo and Goodwyn give them as much as a 12 point advantage. While creating a smarter baby shouldn't be the primary reason to sign with your baby, you can't ignore what researchers have found.

◆ **Higher reading level.** Since one way to reinforce the signs that you'll teach your baby is with books, your baby will look forward to using them more interactively. And speaking of books, research shows that signing children read at a higher level than non-signers. If signing can boost literacy, how can you look the other way?

What's in It for Parents?

Of course all the benefits I've been discussing are reward enough for any loving parent. But isn't it amazing to think that there's personal payback for you, too? Talk about a win-win situation!

◆ You'll enjoy earlier and more meaningful interactions with your baby. Think how amazing and how much fun it'll be to see the world from his perspective.

◆ Your anxiety level will plummet. No need to guess where it hurts or what your baby wants when he's upset. His signs will provide you with specific information about what's going on. That will make the both of you feel better.

◆ You'll even have a brighter future! Face it. The "terrible twos" are inevitable. But fear not, they're not as terrifying for the signing parent! One of the causes of tantrums and other negative behavior such as biting or kicking is a child's inability to communicate. When he can't express himself, it can get ugly. *Your* child, however, will have the ability to sign and can revert to signing when words fail him. Just think how that will improve *your* life.

♦ Getting babysitters will be a snap! When you include grandparents and babysitters in the signing experience, they'll have an easier, more enjoyable time with your baby when you're not there. That means longer and more romantic nights on the town for you and your partner.

♦ Experience more peace and quiet. There will be less crying in your household once your baby learns that signing gets better and faster results than his former routine.

♦ You'll have the knowledge that you have given your baby a gift that lasts a lifetime—and, if you're so inclined, a head-start in learning a second language: American Sign Language (ASL).

Behind the Signs

Today American Sign Language (ASL) is used by more than one million Americans. It's been accepted as a foreign or second language for high school students in California since 1987. College and high school students in over 40 states can now elect sign language as their foreign language.

Bragging About Your Bilingual Baby

The signs you will teach your baby are based on authentic American Sign Language (ASL). While some baby sign language programs suggest that you make up your own signs or use a combination of home-made signs and ASL, your best bet is going with the real thing.

See if you agree with my reasoning. Even if you only use sign language as a way to communicate with your baby before he actually talks, why not use elements of a real language? Who knows, you may want to continue your baby's sign language education beyond his early years. Then you can brag to your friends about having a bilingual child. Of course there's a more practical reason to teach ASL to your baby. It's a standard language that others outside your family will be able to understand.

Decades of research tells us that the period during the first two years of a baby's life is the crucial time to expose him to a second language. Don't miss this window of opportunity!

The Least You Need to Know

♦ Teaching hearing babies to sign is not a new phenomenon. Researchers have been studying it for more than 20 years.

♦ Hearing babies who sign receive a host of emotional, social, language, and cognitive benefits.

♦ Research shows that children who sign also have academic advantages including better literacy skills.

♦ Parents also receive personal benefits when they teach their baby to sign—like more peace and quiet.

♦ Since it's a standard language that many others will be able to understand, teaching your baby American Sign Language (ASL) is your best option.

Chapter 3

Why and How It Works

In This Chapter

- Marvel at how your baby's brain develops
- Learn why your role is vital to the process
- Discover the connection between sign language and the brain
- Recognize the signs that tell you your baby is ready
- Learn when you can expect results

If you're anything like me, you get in the car, turn on the ignition and give absolutely no thought to how you make it from your house to the grocery store and back again. Some of us just take things for granted, I guess. We're trusting souls. We don't care why things work, just that they do.

But because I know that you may be more curious (and lots more skeptical) than I am, let's take a closer look at the idea of teaching your baby to sign and find out exactly why it *does* work. Reverting to the automotive comparison, this chapter will give you an opportunity to kick the tires and look under the hood before you fire up the engine and take that baby out on the open road.

Your Baby's Amazing Brain

Throughout the centuries the brain has been a riddle to scientists. The ancient Greeks were convinced that the *lungs* directed our thoughts, feelings, and emotions. And if you lived in the eighteenth century, "experts" would analyze your skull to find out what was going on in your brain. If you had large temples, you'd have a talent for music. And certain characteristics at the base of your skull told them whether or not you'd make a good parent.

Seems ridiculous, I know, but even today, some questions about the brain go unanswered. Modern techniques have, however, turned up some pretty amazing facts about the brain and in particular, how it develops. What they've found puts an even greater responsibility on parents. Cutting to the chase: the experiences you give your baby during his first years have a *profound* influence on how his brain will develop and his future learning ability.

You Gotta Have Connections

When a baby is born he has about 100 billion nerve cells. According to neurologists, he won't grow any new ones—*ever*. If that's the case then, how does a baby's brain grow after birth? By increasing the number of connections (synapses) between the neurons within his brain.

Each neuron is like a tiny octopus with thousands of tentacles. They carry signals that allow us to hear, see, taste, feel, move, remember, and think. It's where a baby stores information. A baby arrives with a limited number of these responses already intact. He is only capable of hearing, feeling, sucking, and seeing in black and white. Yet within just a few days his brain begins to analyze the outside world. With every experience, with his or your every touch, with every single sound that he hears, another connection in his brain is made. The more the connections, the more the baby is capable of complex thinking.

Behind the Signs

A baby is biologically primed for learning. By age three, a child's brain has twice as many synapses as an adult's. When those connections are used repeatedly in the early years, they become permanent. If not, they don't survive.

That's Some Responsibility!

What does all this mean? Doesn't genetics count for anything any more—aren't Mom and Dad's genes responsible for current and future brain development? Not according to the experts. In fact it looks as if your genes only determine your baby's main circuitry, those that control basic functions like breathing, heartbeat, and reflexes. That means that trillions of connections will be determined by the stimulation that you give your child throughout his early years.

It's incredible information, don't you think? In a nutshell, researchers have found that nurture trumps nature. Yes, genetics is important, but it's not the only thing responsible for your baby's brainpower. It means that your job in creating a smart, successful, and emotionally secure child only started on the night you and your partner got cozy during the blackout. You still have so much work to do!

But it's also exciting, isn't it? To think that the more you offer your child in the way of sensory and educational experiences, the more powerful his brain will become? Not only will these experiences change the physical structure of your baby's brain but they will have a major impact on his intellectual and emotional well-being throughout his entire life. Whew! You've really got your work cut out for you.

Behind the Signs

During the first month of life, the number of connections, or synapses, dramatically increases from 50 trillion to 1 quadrillion. If an infant's body grew at a comparable rate, his weight would increase from 8.5 pounds at birth to 170 pounds at *one month old.*

Don't Panic!

So what's a parent to do? Some are racing out to corner the market on all the developmental DVDs that are out there. Soon their babies will be falling asleep to classical music and waking up just in time for their reading lesson. Does all that stuff work? Could be. But my advice is to relax and save yourself some money. Want my suggestions on ways to build those all-important connections in your baby's brain? Thought you'd never ask:

- Read to your baby. ZAP! Connections are made in his brain.

- Sing to your baby. ZAP! You can almost hear them connect.

- Cuddle your baby. ZAP! More brain stimulation.

- Talk to your baby. ZAP!

- Add visual information at the same time that you're talking, and voilà! It's called *sign language!* ZAP! ZAP! ZAP!

The Sign Language Connection

Beginning to get the picture? But why do I rate sign language above other programs that stimulate a baby's brain potential? Because it's natural, that's why. Babies gesture on their own. I'm not saying that the other programs won't help to stimulate a baby's brain. They probably do, in fact. Any sensory or educational experience will benefit a baby. But the only one that I personally endorse is the one that comes naturally. Plus it's the only one I know that works—communicating with a baby through gestures or signs.

Exactly how does it work? How does sign language stimulate a baby's brain? Pay attention, class, while I take out my pointer.

The left hemisphere of the brain, located on the same side as your left hand, is stimulated by the words you say when you sign. The right side receives and stores the visual information (signs) that you present to your baby.

Take Note

When it comes to brain development, silence is far from golden. If a baby is rarely spoken to during his early years, he will likely have difficulty mastering language skills later in life. While a baby needs to hear as much language as possible during the first three years, it needs to be direct, personal communication. In other words, parking your baby in front of the TV is not a substitute, even if it's PBS.

Then there's the fact that your baby is doing something with his *hands*. That means that he's stimulating his brain with kinetic information and perfecting his fine motor skills at the same time. Simply put, signing with your baby is a multi-sensory experience—and a virtual bonanza for building more of his brain.

It's All in the Timing

There's another important thing that research tells us. It's true in many areas of our lives but especially so in the early stages of your baby's life. It's about the *timing*.

Given what you now know, it shouldn't come as a surprise that babies and young children learn more in their first five years than they will during the rest of their lives. Since most of the wiring or connections in the brain happen during that time, you only have a small window of opportunity to make a major impact. And here's something else you need to know. There are critical windows for developing a baby's potential within that larger five-year window.

A dramatic example is the window for visual development. If by around six months, a baby is not seeing the world around him normally, his vision will never be normal. Equal stimulation through *both* eyes is so important that if a baby with cataracts doesn't have them removed by six months, the risk for ongoing visual impairment or permanent blindness is extraordinarily high.

And then there's a baby's ability to learn language. The critical stage? Birth to three. The more language that's presented to him during those years, the better his vocabulary and language skills will be throughout childhood and even into his adult life. Now, since experts tell us that parents who sign with their babies tend to talk to them more, your baby will be bombarded with aural stimuli in that area—another reason to sign.

When to Introduce Signs

When should you start teaching your baby sign language? As you will soon see, there are many variables—including when his brain is ready to figure it all out.

Most babies begin to make associations around six to seven months. That's when they start to understand that vocalizing gives them power.

They make a sound and you come running. Once that happens, they begin to realize that signing is powerful, too—and that it's much more effective than crying.

A baby learns that when he cries, you'll appear on the scene but you may not give him what he wants, at least not immediately. When he signs, however, he discovers that he gets much better results. If he makes the sign for EAT, he gets a cracker. If he makes the sign for MORE, voilà—instant service!

But before any of that can happen, his cognitive skills must be developed enough to make the association between a certain sign and what it represents. He must also have enough memory to recall the signs and sufficient motor ability to produce them.

Smart Signs

In order for your baby's brain cells to grow and establish stronger connections, they must be exercised. Think of the sign language as one of the "barbells" that will help strengthen the synapses and neural circuitry of his brain.

Now I don't need to tell you that all babies are different. While seven months may be the average age that most babies are first ready to be exposed to signs, not all babies that age will be. Some will be at the starting gate at six months; others, not until 10 months to a year. How can you tell when the time is right for your future signer? Look for clues that he's interested in communicating:

- Does your baby look at your face intently when you speak?

- When your baby drops a toy or some other object, does he look to see where it went?

- Does your baby seem really curious? For example, is he turning his head to see what's going on around him?

- When your baby picks up an object does he look to you quizzically as if he's asking for more information?

- Does your baby point to the objects that he wants?

- Is your baby already gesturing on his own? For example, is he reaching out to be picked up or waving "bye-bye"?

- Can your baby imitate gestures or actions?

If you answered "yes" to five out of seven questions, then it's time for you to get to work. If you answered "no" to the majority of the questions, wait a few weeks and review them again. Remember that babies are making major strides very quickly at this stage so a few weeks can make all the difference.

Manual Dexterity

Want another tip to help determine if your baby is nearing the signing stage? *Look at his hands.* Since a baby's hands must be agile enough to make the signs you are showing him, it's another factor you need to consider. While there are numerous resources available about a baby's developmental stages, there's hardly any focus on how a baby's hands develop.

2 months	A baby's hands start to unfold and briefly hold a rattle.
3 months	He plays with his hands and can hold onto the rattle a little longer.
4 months	He reaches for objects.
5 months	He grabs his toes. His reach is more accurate and he can transfer objects from one hand to the other.
6–9 months	He can pick up small objects with his thumb and finger. He reaches accurately. He can make a sign!
12–15 months	He can grip a crayon.

Jump-Starting the Process

If you've discovered that your baby isn't quite ready to begin, why not put the wait time to good use? Start learning the signs yourself, teach them to your family and be ready when he is. Want an even better idea? Put your baby in training!

Here are some simple activities that will stimulate your baby's interest in sign language, improve his motor skills, and promote his verbal language development at the same time:

◆ Gently manipulate your baby's hands to help him with tasks that he's having trouble with.

◆ Clap to music and songs. Gently take your baby's hands and help him with the movements and gestures.

◆ Play sorting games. Yes, you will have to do most of the work but speak as you play and explain your reasoning to your baby throughout the activity.

◆ Take your baby to a mirror and play "Identification." Touch your nose and say, "This is Mommy's nose." Then touch your baby's nose and say, "This is Amanda's nose." Then move on to your mouth. You get the idea.

◆ Stimulate your baby with "touch and feel" activities. Present him with a number of different textures and let him feel the difference. For example, rub a silk scarf on his hand and then let him feel a scrub brush.

◆ Read to your baby as often as possible. Babies love repetition so limit the number of books that you read to him. Take his finger and help him point to the objects/characters while stressing the name of each.

Smart Signs

If you are not certain if your baby is ready to sign, go ahead and begin. Even if it's too early, the worst that will happen is that it will take you a bit longer to see results.

◆ Play "Peek a Boo." Yes, it's a simple activity, but it's great for developing and maintaining eye contact. That's important when it comes to signing.

When to Expect Results

How soon until you see results? There are variables that you need to factor into the equation. It depends on how old your baby is and how regularly you sign with him, among other things.

While there are no crystal balls in this area, you're probably the persistent type and want a better answer.

The following timetable will help to give you a *general* idea of what to expect and when to expect it. Again, let me stress that this is based on an *average* and doesn't apply in all cases.

3–6 months	While babies are too young to begin any serious signing, this is a good time for you to put your baby in training and jump-start the process. Plus it's a great time for you to practice what you're about to teach.
6–8 months	Your baby's memory skills are growing daily. If you begin signing when your baby is six to seven months old, you will probably see results about two months later. This is based on a high level of commitment and consistency.
8–10 months	Your baby's coordination skills have improved dramatically and he will be able to produce simple signs and begin to grasp their meaning. If you start at this stage, you should see results in six to eight weeks.
10–12 months	If you introduce signs to your baby at this age, you should see results in two to three weeks.
12–18 months	This is a prime imitation period. Watch what you say and watch what you sign. It could be picked up instantly, although the realization of what you're doing and why you're doing it, may take a few days to a week.

Signing Variables

Why can't I be more exact? It's common sense, really. There are just too many variables that need to be considered:

- ◆ **Your baby's age.** The older the baby, the faster he will sign. (Bet you couldn't have figured that out on your own.)

- ◆ **What else is on his mind?** If your baby is learning to crawl or walk, that could delay things for awhile. Babies under nine months are still trying to control their arms and legs. They will learn to sign eventually but they can only do so much all at once. Cut 'em some slack!

♦ **Your baby's mood and interest level.** Your baby may not be interested in what you are teaching him. Try other signs. Or maybe he's just crabby that day.

♦ **Your level of commitment.** The more committed you are to the concept of signing, the faster your baby will begin.

♦ **Your consistency level.** The more you sign with the baby, the faster he will catch on.

♦ **The family's level of involvement.** The more that parents and other family members get involved, the quicker the results.

Rather than worry about *when* your baby will sign, try to have fun with the process. Until your baby shows you that first "sign" of progress, it may get a bit repetitive. But repetition is how your baby will learn. The problem with repetition, however, is that it is often accompanied by its nasty sidekick, boredom. And you simply cannot allow that monster to rear its ugly head!

Don't Give Up!

Dear KinderSigns:

I have been signing with my Billy since he was eight months old. Now he's 11 months old and he's still not signing. I am so frustrated that I am about to give up!

Signed,

Frustrated in Frisco

Dear Frustrated:

Don't you dare! I know that not seeing immediate results can be discouraging, but the benefits for Billy are so remarkable that you can't afford to abandon the effort.

You probably just have a slow signer. One day, maybe even tomorrow, it will happen. When it does, it'll be like someone switched on a 300-watt light bulb over his head. It will be the moment when you (and he) realize that he gets it! He really, really gets it!!

One day soon you'll look at his chubby little hand. You'll see that it's heading for his mouth! Then he'll do it again and you'll realize that Billy wants to EAT.

Then he'll do it faster and maybe give you that impatient look of his. Hurry up, give him a cookie or something! Then he'll make another sign, the one for MORE. There's that impatient look, again. He wants MORE and he wants MORE - now!

The morale of the story? Be careful what you wish for.

P.S. Of course, I jest! You just can't take this thing too seriously. Billy will sign when he's ready. So relax, keep doing what you've been doing and enjoy what your baby is doing today!

Hang in there!

Diane

Now, did I really know why Billy wasn't signing? I hadn't a clue. As I said, there are far too many variables. It could be that he just didn't feel like it.

It's like the story of little Matthew. Normal birth. Normal weight. Normal development. Yet by the time Matthew was three, he hadn't said a word. Naturally, his parents were concerned. They took him to a pediatrician and everything checked out fine. There was just no physical reason why Matthew wasn't talking.

They took him to a speech therapist. She couldn't figure it out either. Matthew celebrated his fourth birthday. And not a sound did he make.

And then it was time for Matthew to go to kindergarten. His mother woke him early so he would have a nice breakfast before boarding the school bus. She opened a box of cereal, a new brand, and put some in his bowl. Matthew took a bite.

All of a sudden, Matthew made a horrific face and spit the cereal on the floor and exclaimed, "That tastes like miserable, stinking garbage! You have some nerve serving me something as disgusting as that!!"

His parents were both thrilled and stunned! "Matthew, My God! You spoke! After all these years, you finally said something. Please tell us, why after all this time did you decide to speak?"

Matthew glared at them with his hands on his hips and said, "Up 'til now, everything's been fine."

So there you have it. The same holds true when it comes to signing. If your baby doesn't feel like it, if you don't give him a reason to sign, it's not gonna happen. You have to make it fun and you have to make it relevant. And some day, like Billy and Matthew, he'll get it. He'll really, really get it.

The Least You Need to Know

♦ A baby's brain is a work in progress. How smart he will be goes beyond genetics and it depends to an even greater degree on the varied experiences he gets between birth and five.

♦ Sign language stimulates both side of the brain and promotes greater brain function.

♦ There is no exact age to determine when your baby is ready to sign but there are signs you can look for to determine if he's ready to begin.

♦ Results of your signing efforts depend on many variables including the baby's age and how often you sign with him.

2

Ready, Set, Sign!

Now that you have a basic understanding of what's involved with teaching your baby to sign, it's almost time to take this show on the road. Have a case of opening night jitters? That's understandable. After all, this is uncharted territory for you. But take my advice, relax and have fun. Signing with your baby should be as natural as speaking to him. You really can't make any mistakes. Even if you don't follow my advice to the letter, the worst thing that could happen is that it'll take your baby a little longer to catch on. And who knows? You may discover some techniques that work even better than mine.

In Part 2, you'll learn what to do to get started. Follow the guidelines as closely as possible and add your own personality and creativity to the mix. Did you notice that I said "guidelines?" Since you know your baby better than anyone, you should adopt what works and adapt what doesn't. Keep in mind that your baby not only needs to learn signs, he needs to make associations. And you need to do whatever you can to make it all happen.

Ready? Okay, here we go. Fasten your seatbelts. It's going to be a thrilling ride!

Chapter 4

Introducing Baby's First Signs

In This Chapter

- ◆ Discover the difference between iconic and abstract signs
- ◆ Find out which signs to teach first
- ◆ Learn how to teach other important signs
- ◆ Look for signs of progress

Kudos to you for getting this far and making the right decision. You may have been skeptical at first, but you read the background, studied the research, and came to the conclusion that teaching your baby to sign was something too good to pass up.

So what are you waiting for? Wake up that lazy child and tell him that the school bell is about to ring! Well, maybe you should give him another hour in the sack. Because first, you have to learn how to teach him.

Sign Language Categories

I know you're anxious to get going but would you mind putting every-thing in neutral for a few minutes more? There's a bit of technical infor-mation that you need to know before we're off and running. It may seem a bit bothersome now, but believe me, it'll make things go more smoothly down the road. It has to do with the two types of signs that you'll teach your baby:

- ◆ **Iconic signs.** These are signs that mimic the action or the look of what you're trying to communicate. Iconic signs are the easiest for you to teach and for your baby to learn. Take the sign for TELE-PHONE, for example. You already know how to make that iconic sign. It's just like you thought. Thumb to your ear, pinky finger to your mouth.

- ◆ **Abstract signs.** These signs are a little harder to teach because their meanings can't be conveyed by a simple gesture. To teach them you'll need to create an association so your baby will make the connection. It sounds more complicated than it is. You'll under-stand better in our first example, the sign for MORE.

The First Three Signs: MORE, EAT, and MILK

The first signs you'll teach are MORE, EAT, and MILK. They've been chosen because they're important concepts to your little one. In fact, in the earliest stages, they're pretty much all that he cares about. He wants something to eat, something to wash it down with, and more of both. Another reason they work well is that none of them look alike. They won't confuse your baby—or you.

MORE is the very first sign that your baby will learn. It's also the most important sign since it will serve as the foundation for all others. Once your baby understands the concept of MORE and can make the sign (or even come close), the other signs will come quickly.

Important Note: If your baby is less than 12 months old, stick with this sign until he masters it. It will be less confusing for him and you'll see results faster. Once he gets it, move on to the other two signs. If your baby is a year or more, introduce all three signs, but not at the same time, of course.

The Sign for MORE

Put the tips of your fingers together a few times.

Even though it's an abstract concept, MORE is a sign that babies learn very quickly. Oftentimes, it's their very first *spoken* word. It's also a good starter sign because there are many different opportunities to teach it throughout the day. In other words, *you* won't get bored.

Your baby can use this sign to ask for *more* food, *more* juice, or *more* pages of the book that you're reading to him. All he has to do is put the tips of his fingers together and "ask."

Behind the Signs

The average baby will eat 15 pounds of cereal in his first year. That's great news when you consider there's an opportunity to teach EAT and MORE with your baby's every spoonful.

Techniques to Teach MORE

1. When you're feeding your baby, give him a few teaspoons from that jar of green beans or whatever the "daily special" might be.

Then stop cold. Before he can get upset, make the sign for MORE and ask, "MORE? Do you want MORE?"

Continue this throughout the meal, making sure that there are enough "feeding stoppages" so the idea begins to register. Repeat this pattern frequently throughout every meal, stressing the word MORE while you sign. Use an expressive and upbeat tone of voice. Smile and make a game of it. Eventually your baby will make the association if you keep repeating the routine. Like learning anything new, repetition is essential.

2. Grab a handful of Cheerios. While your baby's in his high chair, put one on his tray. When he picks it up and pops it in his mouth, ask/sign, "MORE?" Then quickly place another one in front of him. As soon as he eats it, be ready to have another one magically appear, remembering to reinforce the idea by signing and speaking every time.

3. Read a book to your baby. (Babies love to hear your voice and look at the pictures no matter how young they are.) Stop at certain intervals, look at your baby and ask/sign if he wants MORE. Repeat this several times throughout the reading session, always asking, "MORE? Do you want me to read MORE?"

4. Play Peek-a-Boo. It's always a baby-pleaser. Stop every so often and ask/sign MORE. Then resume playing the game. Then do it again and again. And again.

Take Note

When teaching MORE, be careful not to deprive your baby of food or anything else for too long a period. After all, you don't want to torment your child! Your goal is to get him to make the connection between the sign for MORE and actually getting MORE of something that he wants. Learning has to be fun!

5. Play Baby Toss-Up. All babies love it. Pick him up and toss him gently in the air and wait for the belly laughs to begin. Then stop and ask if he wants MORE. Repeat the activity.

6. Gather around the kitchen table with your baby watching from his high chair or from someone's lap. Ask family members if they would like MORE of something. Exaggerate the effort. Have them respond (and sign) that they would. Then place MORE on their plates.

7. Get creative. Think of other ways to teach MORE and then vary them. Make it a family project and remember to relax and have a good time.

The Sign for EAT

Move your hand back and forth to your mouth as if you're eating.

Our next sign is a simple one. It's the sign for EAT. To learn it, your baby will have to make another association. But since the sign for EAT pantomimes someone actually eating something (iconic), it's one that is easy to teach and easy for everyone to remember.

Techniques to Teach EAT

1. It's suppertime and your baby is in his high chair watching you prepare his food. You can tell by his behavior that he's excited about the prospect of eating. Sit down in front of him with a bowl of his favorite strained vegetables and *before* you begin to feed him, ask/sign,

Behind the Signs

Did you know that 10 to 13 percent of the world's population is left-handed? So are 22 percent of all twins. Researchers say it's decided in the womb as early as 10 weeks. What's the connection? It doesn't matter which hand you sign with. Right or left, just keep it consistent.

"EAT? Would you like to EAT?" Again, your voice is upbeat and you are smiling. This has to be fun!

By the way, did you notice the difference between EAT and MORE? With EAT you make the sign several times *before* feeding your baby. Why is that? It's common sense, really. If you stop and start throughout the meal to teach the sign, your baby will get EAT and MORE confused.

2. You don't have to wait until your baby is in the high chair to help him make the association. When you get him out of his crib and dressed before breakfast, make the sign for EAT *before* you leave the room, asking him if he is hungry and ready to EAT his cereal. Then make sure you take him *directly* to the high chair so he makes the connection. On your way there, ask/sign that same question a few more times. Remember to speak when you sign. No exceptions.

3. Surprise your baby at other times of the day by asking him if he would like something to EAT. Repeat the question a few times, and then produce a cracker so the meaning is reinforced.

4. Use whatever props you can think of to reinforce the sign and its association. For example, feed the dog, a family member, or offer a pretend-snack to a stuffed bear.

The Sign for MILK

Your hand opens and closes as if you were milking a cow. Alternate: Many nursing moms use the sign for NURSE. It's made by quickly brushing your hand over your breast in a downward motion.

When you introduce the sign for MILK, you have a different kind of association to make. MILK is something your baby can see and touch (a bottle or a breast).

Techniques to Teach MILK

1. *Before* you give your baby his bottle or your breast, you will ask/sign, "MILK? Would you like some MILK?" Follow the same method as with the previous sign, repeating the question a few times. Then give him the bottle or breast.

2. Now you have another opportunity to help your baby make the association. *During* his feeding, while his attention is focused on you, reinforce the sign by asking/signing, "MILK? Do you like MILK?" While it may be difficult to feed your baby and sign at the same time, ask your spouse or other family member to sign and say MILK/NURSE while your baby is feeding, making sure the sign is made within your baby's sight line.

> **Take Note**
>
> A few weeks after you have introduced a sign to your baby, take your baby's hands and gently shape them to form the sign. Be careful not to force your baby to do this. Just do it occasionally, as a way of encouraging your baby to imitate you.

Teaching Other Important Signs

One of the reasons babies enjoy signing is that it helps them feel good about themselves. They begin to gain a sense of independence. At last they have some control over what's going on. Why they can even provide you with specific information about how you're not measuring up! But only if they have the signs they need at their disposal, of course.

While I've already stated that you should adapt these guidelines to meet your own goals, would you mind if I made one *strong suggestion?* In the beginning stages, teach your baby the signs that he (and you) really need. In other words, teach him the following signs *before* you venture into the good manners and good grooming categories. You can always show him the sign for "toothbrush" next week.

The Sign for HURT/PAIN

*Bring the tips of your index
fingers together a few times.*

The sign for HURT/PAIN is one of the most important signs you can
teach your baby. Once he learns this sign, not only will he be able to
tell you when he's in pain but also where it hurts. Instead of simply crying, your baby will have a valuable tool to help him communicate the
source of his pain. He'll simply make the sign at the place on his body
where it hurts. The bad news is that
in order to learn the sign for HURT/
PAIN, your baby must make the
association between the sign and
pain itself. Unfortunately he'll have
many opportunities to learn first-
hand when he's crawling and starting
to walk.

> **Smart Signs**
>
> It doesn't matter what
> word you use: *Hurt, Pain,
> Boo-Boo,* and *Ow-ie* all
> work fine. Just remember that
> consistency is essential, so
> select one and stick with it.

Techniques to Teach HURT/PAIN

1. When your baby has stubbed his toe or bumped his head, give
   him some cuddles and comfort and, of course, make sure that it's
   only a superficial injury. Then while you're soothing him, make
   the sign for HURT/PAIN where it hurts. If he injures his knee,
   for example, make the sign in front of his knee, saying sympatheti-
   cally, "Did you HURT yourself? Does it HURT? I'm sorry it

HURTS." Remember to stress the word HURT each time, always signing at the point of injury.

2. If the injury is outside your baby's line of vision (e.g. nose, forehead etc.), gently touch/ rub the spot where he was hurt and then make the sign for HURT at that same location on your own body. Make sure, of course, that he's paying attention and not still totally focused on his pain. Repeat this several times, talking to him soothingly. Another alternative is to take him to a mirror so he can see you make the sign at his own nose or forehead. That will help him make a more personal connection.

3. Pretend to hurt yourself while your baby is watching. Bump your knee, for example, then over-react by hopping around, gritting your teeth while making the sign for HURT at your "injury."

   Another time, pretend to walk into a wall and hit your nose. Over-dramatize the situation each time signing and yelling "HURT" as your baby watches from his ringside seat. By the way, all babies really enjoy this activity. The heartless little creatures get a real chuckle out of someone else's suffering.

4. Use a teddy bear as a "crash dummy" and have him injure his head or paw. Then make the sign where he was hurt and top it off with a colorful band-aid to reinforce the point.

The Sign for HELP

Pat your chest with your palms open a few times. (Note: This sign has been adapted from American Sign Language [ASL] to make it easier for a baby to produce. The authentic ASL sign is also included in our dictionary.)

HELP is another sign you'll want your baby to learn. Not only will it eliminate a considerable amount of crying and frustration on your baby's part, but some of your own as well. You won't have to guess what's wrong with him when he starts to cry. Is he hungry? Tired? Teething? No, he wants HELP!

Techniques to Teach HELP

1. Look for situations where your child may actually need help; for example, his older brother takes his toy truck or rattle. He starts to whimper. You come over and ask/sign, "HELP? Do you want HELP?" Then do whatever needs doing to rectify the situation.

2. Watch your child at play. If you notice a situation where you think he may need help, go to him and ask/sign, "Do you want Mommy to HELP?" If he indicates in any way that he *doesn't*, then back off. Remember, you're not only trying to teach him sign language, you also want him to learn independence.

3. Since situations where your baby needs help may not occur frequently enough for him to make the necessary association, you need to get creative again with some edu-tainment. Keep the plot simple, remembering that you are playing to an audience of one.

As with HURT/PAIN, it's important that your baby sees your little HELP vignettes played against different backdrops. You don't want to bore him with the same storyline week after week, do you? Once again you will have to sacrifice your dignity for the greater good, but things are improving. At least you won't have to walk into any walls.

Ready for your close-up? Don't be shy, now. The more of a hambone you are, the faster your baby will learn. Get ready for what I like to call the "Academy Award" technique. ACTION!

"As the Bowl Crashes"

Starring: Mary Sunshine, her swashbuckling husband Rex, and their son Baby Boswell

Setting: An ordinary kitchen in Middle America. The family is gathered around the table. Baby Boswell is in his high chair taking in all the action.

Direction: Mary reaches for a bowl on a very high shelf and can't get it. She exaggerates her plight, signing as she cries for HELP!!!

> Mary: Rex, can you HELP? I need HELP getting this bowl down from the shelf. Please come and HELP!! Oh, won't someone HELP!!!

> Rex: Mary, did you say you needed HELP? I would be glad to HELP. Why didn't you call for HELP sooner?

> Mary: Oh, Rex, you're such a big HELP—and my hero!

THE END

Here's another reason to vary these rescue scenes. If you repeat the above scenario too often, your baby is liable to make the sign for HELP when he wants a BOWL.

The Sign for DIAPER CHANGE

All fingers except the thumb curl into your palms. Your knuckles rest against each other and pivot in opposite directions. (Note: The sign for DIAPER CHANGE is actually the sign for CHANGE with "diaper" implied.)

Can a baby really "tell" you when he needs his diaper changed? Yes, if he wants to. With today's disposable diapers, your baby may not feel uncomfortable and not mind being wet or messy. Yet there are babies who *abhor* the feeling and would be thrilled to have a more efficient way to call for personal valet service.

DIAPER CHANGE is not as essential as the other signs but since it may benefit your baby, why not give it a try and see what happens?

Take Note

Some babies really hate having their diaper changed so this sign may not be one of their favorites. In fact, if you ask/sign if they want a DIAPER CHANGE, some toddlers may run the other way. If that happens, don't waste your time with this sign. Babies will only learn the signs they're interested in.

Techniques to Teach DIAPER CHANGE

When you introduce the sign for DIAPER CHANGE, your goal is to get your baby to communicate when he's uncomfortable and wants you to change his diaper. In order for your baby to make this association, he needs to be aware of the process of having his diaper taken off and on. Your reactions when you actually change his diaper will help to reinforce that awareness.

1. When a baby has a wet or soiled diaper, make a big deal about changing it. Because the sign requires two hands, put your baby on a blanket on the floor or some other safe place. Then say/sign, "DIAPER CHANGE? Do you want your DIAPER CHANGED?" Repeat this a few times making sure you stress the words DIAPER CHANGE as well as the sign.

2. Remove your baby's diaper, all the while saying/signing something like "You really needed a DIAPER CHANGE!" or "A DIAPER CHANGE is my favorite thing to do."

3. Once the diaper is off and your baby is clean, let him go *au naturel* for a while allowing him to feel the cool air on his bottom.

4. While he is still in the buff, play the "Diaper Game!" Place a diaper behind you or somewhere out of your baby's sight. Then say/sign, "Where is the DIAPER? Pretend to look around you asking the same question. Keep repeating it and signing. Then magically bring the diaper into your baby's sight line as you enthusiastically say/sign, "Here's the DIAPER! We found the DIAPER!"

You can also diaper a teddy bear or baby doll to help your baby make the association. In fact, using a "stand-in" (real or otherwise) works well in teaching many of the signs. In this case, don't ask for human volunteers. Family cooperation will only go so far.

Behind the Signs

According to behavioral experts, men are faster than women when it comes to changing diapers. Research shows that the average woman takes 2 minutes and 5 seconds. Men can take a diaper off (and put it back on) in 1 minute and 36 seconds! One expert says it's because men think of it like a mechanical process and want to get it over with as quickly as possible. (Like women *don't*?)

Looking for Signs of Progress

Okay, let's say that you have been signing for a month or two and nothing is happening. If you think that your baby should be making better progress (based on all the variables we discussed earlier), there are some things you can do to determine if you're making any headway.

1. Say a target word (MORE, EAT, etc.) *without* making the sign. Pay close attention to see if your baby's eyes travel down to your hands. If so, it means that he is used to receiving information verbally *and* visually. You are definitely making progress.

2. Give him another test. Place your baby's bottle on the floor with a few other objects. Then watch him carefully as you sign and say MILK. If he looks to the bottle, congratulations, you are really getting close. Try the same thing with a diaper, a book, or other object signs you are trying to teach.

3. Keep in mind that your idea of progress might not be the same as your baby's. His signs may not look like yours at first. It takes lots of dexterity to make some of them perfectly. In fact, your baby may already be signing and you may not even know it!

Recognizing Early Attempts

How will you be able to figure out what your baby is trying to sign to you in the beginning stages? No, his signs may not replicate yours exactly, but he *is* doing his best and should be rewarded for his efforts. So pay close attention!

Be on the lookout for any motions or gestures that seem out of the ordinary, especially if your baby keeps repeating them. If you still can't figure out what your baby is trying to communicate, look around you. Chances are it has something to do with the current situation or nearby object. Like any good detective, survey the scene.

If you're still stymied, it may help to know more about the first attempts of other babies:

- ◆ **MORE.** Some babies clap their hands together. Others close their fists and tap them together when they want MORE of something.

- ◆ **EAT.** There are babies who put their hand or fist in their mouth or point to their mouth with one finger when they want something to EAT.

- ◆ **MILK.** A thirsty baby may wave or shake his hand or even reach out toward your bottle or breast for MILK.

Smart Signs

When your baby approximates a sign, show him that you're pleased with the effort but then demonstrate the correct way to do it. Don't imitate his attempt. As your baby's fine motor skills improve, so will his ability to make the sign properly. Give him something to strive for!

Do what you can to identify what your baby is trying to communicate to you. Once you do, lavish him with praise—while showing the correct sign as you say something like, "Yes, Tommy! You want MILK? Aren't you the smartest boy, telling Daddy that you want MILK? Now, can you sign SKIM or TWO PERCENT?"

The Least You Need to Know

♦ The first signs you will introduce to your baby are MORE, EAT, and MILK.

♦ MORE is the most important sign and the foundation for all other signs.

♦ If your baby is under 12 months, wait until he masters MORE before you introduce any other signs. If your baby is over 12 months, introduce MORE, EAT, AND MILK at the same time.

♦ HURT and HELP are important signs for your baby to learn.

♦ Your baby may not be interested in the sign for DIAPER CHANGE but it's worth giving it a try.

♦ Be on the lookout for signs of progress. A unfamiliar gesture could be a first attempt at signing.

Chapter 5

Increasing Your Baby's Sign Language Vocabulary

In This Chapter

- ◆ Learn to teach two helpful signs
- ◆ Do some planning and set some goals
- ◆ Explore signing opportunities
- ◆ Discover how to combine signs
- ◆ Learn how to sign in sentences

So far, so good? I told you it was going to be easier than you thought. In fact, if you've taught your baby all the signs in the previous chapter, you don't really have to go any further! Many parents are content with just providing the basic signs.

If you decide to stop now, you and your baby will still reap many of the rewards that I talked about earlier. However, you'll miss out on even greater benefits and lots more fun. So don't be a quitter! Hang in there! You've gotten through the hard part. From here on in, it's smooth sailing. And I'm here to guide you every step of the way.

Helpful Signs to Teach

Some signs are more important to parents and caregivers than they are to babies. DON'T TOUCH and GENTLE TOUCH are two of them.

DON'T TOUCH is a combination of the sign for NO and the sign for TOUCH. As you might imagine, once your baby begins to roam, it's a sign that you'll use frequently. Will it help him to communicate his wants and needs? No, it won't. As a matter of fact, there's a good chance that your baby would prefer that you didn't learn these signs at all!

So why teach them? Because you're a good parent, of course, and want to keep your baby safe. Learning DON'T TOUCH, for instance, will help you add emphasis to your verbal instructions. As your little one gets older, it can also be one of your "secret signs." When you're in a high-end shop, for example, and he reaches for that Waterford vase, you can simply flash the sign and you won't have to reprimand him in public. (Just to be on the safe side, I'd grab the vase first and then make the sign.)

The Sign for DON'T TOUCH

DON'T TOUCH is a combination of NO and TOUCH. Your index and middle fingers snap to the thumb (NO), then your middle finger taps the back of the other hand (TOUCH).

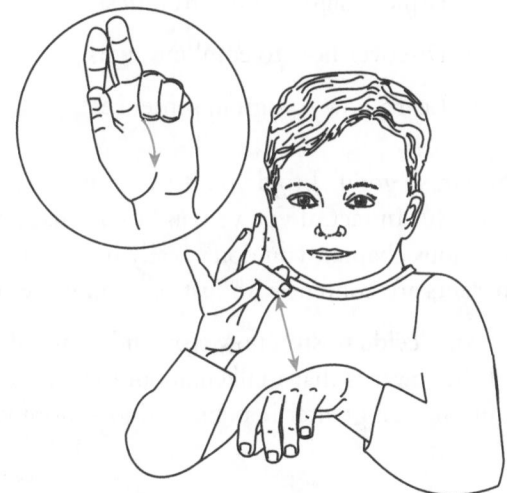

Techniques to Teach DON'T TOUCH

1. Just as with any other sign, your baby needs to make an association. When you see him touching something that he shouldn't, quickly grab his hand, make eye contact, and show him the sign while shaking your head and sternly saying "DON'T TOUCH."

   As I said earlier, this will not be your baby's favorite sign but it will help you keep him out of harm's way. Just remember the four components that are necessary to get your message across: the tone of your voice, your stern facial expression, your spoken words, and the sign itself.

2. Play "The Untouchables Game." You can begin teaching this sign to your baby the fun way and then get serious later on.

   Spread some objects in a row on the floor. Five or six will do. It doesn't matter what they are but one should be different in some way from the rest. For example, line up some of your baby's picture books and one of your own thick bestsellers. Or try five stuffed toys and one wooden one.

   Then touch each object, saying with a happy voice and a smile "Touch. Touch. Touch. Touch. Touch." When you get to the hardcover book, begin to touch it but quickly pull your hand away. At the same time make a noticeable frown and say in a much deeper voice, "DON'T TOUCH!" and make the sign. Vary the sequence so the "untouchable" object isn't always at the end. After you do this a few times, take your baby's hand and gently guide him through the same activity.

   If you play this "game" enough, your baby will make the association plus he'll think it's an absolute riot—until you play it for real. Sure it's a bit underhanded, but remember that it's for your baby's safety.

Smart Signs

When you're teaching a sign, use every tool you can think of to help your baby make an association. Voice and body language should be at the top of the list. The look on your face, the tone of your voice, and your general demeanor will help to convey vital information.

3. Another idea is to walk your baby around the kitchen touching different things while happily saying, "Touch. Touch. Touch." When you get to the stove or toaster, begin to reach out to touch them, then quickly pull your hand away, lower your voice, make a stern face and say/sign "DON'T TOUCH!" This activity should be "played" more seriously than the previous version using the books or toys, since these are objects that you *really* don't want him to touch.

The Sign for GENTLE TOUCH

One hands gently "pets" the back of the other hand.

Another valuable sign is GENTLE TOUCH. Basically, it's one hand "petting" the back of the other hand, as if you were stroking a cat. And, speaking of cats, that's one of the reasons this sign is important.

If you have a cat or other pet in your home or are visiting a friend who has one, your baby's first inclination may be to grab or squeeze it. With the GENTLE TOUCH sign, you can teach him to be kind and gentle in his manner of touch. The soothing tone of your voice as you "pet" your hand will help convey its meaning. The sign is also useful when holding delicate objects or when visiting friends with younger babies than yours.

Techniques to Teach GENTLE TOUCH

1. Touch your baby, rubbing his arm or leg while saying slowly and soothingly, "GENTLE TOUCH. GENTLE TOUCH."

2. Get out the props. Use a teddy bear or draft a live family volunteer and while your baby is watching, rub the subject's arm while speaking and signing, "GENTLE TOUCH."

3. If you have a family pet, pet him gently, guiding your baby's hand over his fur while saying and signing "GENTLE TOUCH."

Where Do You Go From Here?

Okay, time for a breather. You've worked hard and learned a lot in a very short time. Some of you may have already put that knowledge to the test and have started to sign with your baby. Others are scrutinizing their little ones looking for signs that they're ready to begin. And for those of you who are waiting for the stork to land, you couldn't have picked a better time to learn. Things are about to get a bit more hectic in your household.

No matter where you are in the process, I'm glad that you're sticking with me. But before you determine what the next step will be, you need to ask yourself what you're trying to accomplish—and set some goals. First think long-term.

> **Take Note**
>
> Even if you choose not to introduce some signs to your baby, he may still pick them up by "osmosis." For example, don't be surprised one day when you tell your baby to do something and he looks at you and signs, NO!

Do you want your baby to become skilled in sign language and use it into early childhood, maybe even as an adult? If that's your goal, keep in mind that this is *baby* sign language and it's as basic as it gets. It's a way for a child to communicate what he wants and feels in a very limited way. While this is a great place to start, if you are really serious about teaching sign language as a second language, a more comprehensive and structured approach is necessary.

If, however, you're like most parents and want to use sign language solely as a communication bridge before your baby can express himself with words, you need to decide which signs to teach after you've introduced the basics. No one can do it for you. After all, would you want someone to tell you what words your baby should say? Well, no one should tell you what *signs* to teach either.

To help you establish your signing goals, ask yourself which signs would be most helpful to your baby in expressing himself. Also ask what would be helpful to you in understanding what he wants or feels. And don't forget the fun factor! Think about what signs your baby could learn just for the sheer delight of it.

To help you decide, look at the signs in the Baby Sign Language Dictionary, which appears in the middle of this book. They are authentic ASL signs and are the most popular with parents since they are all relevant to a baby's world. Review the different categories and decide which ones you'd like your baby to learn. Family signs, perhaps? That would be helpful. Good manners? A good choice. Animal signs? Always crowd-pleasers. Regardless of your decision, keep in mind that the goals you set are simply *guidelines* to help you establish some direction. Keep them flexible. You'll soon learn why.

> **Behind the Signs**
>
> Most parents consider baby sign language as an interim method of communication and teach between 10 and 20 signs. How long you sign with your baby and how many signs you teach is up to you. Research shows that even a limited exposure to sign language will benefit your baby.

Introducing Additional Signs

If you're ready to move ahead, it means that your baby has mastered the basics. He's come to realize that gestures have meaning. He's knows that when he makes a particular sign, he gets something that he wants. By now, you've reviewed all the signs and have decided which signs you want to add to your baby's signing vocabulary. But *how* and *when* do you teach him?

Let me answer that question with another question. How would you go about introducing new *spoken* words to your child's vocabulary?

Hmmm. Hard to put into words, isn't it? That's because teaching your baby to speak is something that *just comes naturally*. You talk, your baby listens and he imitates what he hears. If your baby sees something that he's interested in, he'll stare at it, pick it up or point to it. You react by slowly saying the name of whatever he's interested in and by repeating the word so he remembers it.

Well, teaching your baby new signs isn't that different, really. The only difference is that when you say the word, you now add a sign. All it takes is a little pre-planning, some common sense, and a keen eye.

Identifying Signing Opportunities

Let's say that you've decided to teach your baby all the signs in the clothing category. Keeping in mind that he must make an association before he can learn any of them, when do you think the ideal time would be to teach him? Bingo! Of course, it's when you're getting him dressed in the morning and undressed at night. Going for a walk outside? Teach him the signs for HAT and COAT.

Interested in teaching your baby good manners? Mealtime would be a good place to start. What about animal signs? Use his favorite animal picture book. Analyze your daily routine. You're sure to discover many teaching opportunities right in front of you.

> **Take Note**
>
> Babies love repetition. It not only makes them feel comfortable when they're able to predict outcomes, it makes them feel more in control. The problem is that while babies *love* repetition, adults don't. So try to vary the signing routines and come up with different ways to help your baby make the necessary associations. You can't afford to get bored!

The important thing to remember is to make your teaching relevant. Always *sign in context*. It's critical that your baby associate some real meaning to the signs you are showing him. And since he won't figure it all out immediately, you need to make the signs and reinforce the associations repeatedly.

Creating Your Own Opportunities

There is a major resource available to you when it comes to introducing and reinforcing signs you want your baby to learn. It's something that's jam-packed with ongoing teaching opportunities. It's called *life*.

Look around you. Life is a signing classroom. Take your "student" on a few field trips. Even your back yard is an adventure to a baby. Just open the door and point to what you see, say the word and make the sign. What about a trip to the zoo? What a great opportunity to teach animal signs! And what better way to teach family member signs than hauling out the family photo album?

Following Your Baby's Lead

Another way (and the very best way) to figure out what signs to teach your baby is to *take the lead from him*. Yes, your baby can and will tell you what he wants to learn, if you pay attention.

Remember those goals that I helped you set a few paragraphs ago and my advice to keep them flexible? I made that suggestion because your baby may have a different signing philosophy than you do.

Let's say, for example, you're sitting on a blanket in the backyard trying to teach your baby the sign for BOOK. All of a sudden, he throws down the book, looks up, and points to a BIRD. If that happens, it's a priceless opportunity to teach him a sign! In effect he's saying, "I'm not at all intrigued by that silly book. But I *am* really interested in that thing up there. What is it? Can you give me more information?"

What should you do when that happens? You have two choices:

1. You can say, "Sorry. This is inconsistent with the goals that I have established for you to reach today. Animal signs are one week from Tuesday."

2. Or you can keep your goals flexible, seize the moment and say, "Oh, a BIRD (sign)! Look at that beautiful BIRD. Look, there's another BIRD."

Of course, you'll choose #2. It's common sense and good salesmanship. It reminds me of a recent trip I made to Morocco, when the merchant in a gift shop followed my every eye movement. When I glanced at a brass plate, he presented it to me before I uttered a single word. Wouldn't it have been foolish of him to bring me a stuffed camel when I was coveting a plate? (I wound up buying both, but that's beside the point.)

Being Prepared

To promote baby-driven signing opportunities like the one I just mentioned, *let your child explore*. Be prepared with as many signs as you can ahead of time. If he picks up a diaper, be ready with the sign for DIAPER CHANGE. If he picks up a sneaker, present him with the sign for SHOE. If he points to the TELEPHONE, your baby wants to know more about it. (Or else he wants you to order a pizza.) Give him more information! Tell him the name of the object and show him the sign.

As you can see, it's really helpful to know specific signs ahead of time. Review the signs in the middle of this book and practice those that are likely to come up. Since many of the signs are iconic—they mimic the action or the look of what you're trying to communicate—you'll have an easy time remembering them. Learn a few more each day and you'll be an expert in no time.

But what happens if your baby picks something up and you don't know the sign? Don't panic! While it would be a shame to miss out on a signing opportunity, there will be other chances. Just remember to look up that sign and be ready the next time.

But, in the interest of full disclosure, there is another school of thought as to what you should do if you don't know a sign. *Make one up.*

Remember the *Baby Signs* program we talked about in Chapter 1? In it Professors Acredolo and Goodwyn suggest that you invent your own sign in a situation like that. Their advice is to create a simple gesture that represents the look or idea of the object. For example, if you don't know the sign for DOG, consider panting like one.

Smart Signs

How quickly you introduce new signs depends on your baby. Introduce one or two new signs and see how fast he catches on. Once your baby figures out that by making gestures, his life will get easier, he'll soak up new signs like a sponge. Even if you give him more than he can handle, he'll eventually figure it out.

Whether or not you should follow that strategy depends on your over-all objective. If you want your baby to take American Sign Language seriously, then pass up the opportunity, look up the legitimate ASL sign and be ready the next time. If your objective is shorter-term and you don't plan on teaching your baby any more signs after he learns to talk, then you might give it a try. *It's important to remember*, however, that others may not be able to identify the signs you created on your own, because they're not part of any standard sign language. If it were me, I'd stick with ASL.

Your Baby's Own Inventions

In Chapter 1, you learned how Linda Acredolo became inspired to study this subject in the first place. If you recall, it was when her daughter Kate spontaneously began to make up her own signs. Her sign for FISH was to blow, since there was a fish mobile over her crib and her mom had to blow on it to make it move. To Kate, sniffing and wiggling her nose meant FLOWER because she saw people doing something similar when they picked one from the garden.

So what do you do if your baby makes up his own sign? Babies are very smart and creative, you know, and it's possible that yours may create a sign that's not in the dictionary. What to do? Well, you could ignore his effort and pretend you didn't notice. Not a great idea, right? Or you could get excited, praise him for his creativity and respond by giving him what he wants or show that you understand in some other way. Sound like a better plan? I agree.

But then you have to make another decision. Do you incorporate your baby's invented sign into your sign language lexicon or do you respond by showing him the actual sign that you want him to learn? When you think about it, it's pretty much the same quandary you had when your baby asked you for a sign and you didn't know it. Again, it's really your call and depends on how much of an American Sign Language purist you are and want your child to become.

There's one really important thing you need to keep in mind if you do opt to continue to use your baby's own signs. Be sure to record it some-where and let your family and other caregivers know about it. Nothing will dampen your baby's enthusiasm for signing like not being under-stood by everyone.

Pacing Yourself

How fast do you introduce new signs? Why not find the person in charge and get his input? Guess who that might be? Right. The one in the crib.

Again look to your baby for guidance. See if he's interested. If he's not, try again at another time. Just don't bombard him with too much information all at once. As a parent, you'll be able to figure it out. Trust your instincts. No one can read him like you can.

If your baby "asks" for a word/sign by looking or pointing at something, tell him what it is and, if it's relevant, show him the sign. If another opportunity presents itself, go for it. Keep using the signs that your baby already knows so they stay fresh in his memory and introduce new ones when it feels like it's the right thing to do. Keep it fun and keep it natural.

I've said this before but it bears repeating: Teach sign language the same way you teach your baby to speak. You're not concerned about *talking* to your baby too much, are you? Does he understand every single word that you say to him? Of course not, but that doesn't stop you from talking. In fact, the more you talk, the better his vocabulary will become. It's the same with signing. Your baby has an amazing brain. He will eventually sort it all out.

Behind the Signs

Whenever you offer a new word/sign to your baby, another connection within the brain is made. Words are stored on the left side of the brain and visual information (signs) is stored on the right side. The more you speak and sign to your baby, the more his brain is stimulated.

Combining Signs

While putting more than one sign together isn't essential to your baby's signing success, if you want him to matriculate to the advanced class, by all means, give it a try. Again use the common sense approach. Do I really need to tell you, for example, not to combine two signs when your baby hasn't mastered one?

Sometimes your baby may make combinations on his own. Maybe he'll sign MORE and MILK when he wants a refill. Be prepared and be impressed when that happens!

If he doesn't combine signs on his own initiative, offer some encouragement. EAT and MORE would be a good starting combo. Just be certain that your baby understands *both* signs and *both* concepts. Common sense, again. Then follow the same techniques as you used when introducing other signs, keeping in mind that repetition plus consistency equals success.

By the time a baby reaches the stage when he's combining signs, he should be saying at least a few words. Make sure that your efforts are now even more focused on his verbal development. Use signs as a secondary means of support and motivation.

Signing in Sentences

There's another way of looking at signing combinations. You might even think of them as baby *sentences!* When a baby signs DOG and BALL he's really saying "The dog has a ball." If he signs EAT and ALL DONE, he is telling you that he can't eat another bite. While he obviously has a long way to go before he can embark on a career in the Senate, these combinations represent a major stride in the way a baby is thinking. Putting two concepts together is a big deal for any baby. So lavish him with praise and cheer him on!

By the way, don't expect any signing combinations much before 18 months and maybe much later. They almost always happen when a baby should be speaking. That's why many babies use a combination of the two, making a sign and saying a word.

> **Take Note**
>
> Don't panic or express disappointment if your baby doesn't sign in a particular situation when he may have signed in that same situation before. He may simply not be in the mood. *You* don't always feel like talking, do you? Try to motivate him with a happy face and a few signing repetitions. If nothing happens, there's always tomorrow.

Your Little Conversationalist

In his book, *Sign with Your Baby* (see Appendix C), Joseph Garcia talks about a time when one of his sons actually started a conversation by making a sign. According to Garcia, he and his sons had seen a few airplanes the day before and had fun making the sign whenever they saw one. A few days later while in his high chair, one son started making the AIRPLANE sign. Garcia was puzzled since there were obviously no airplanes landing in the kitchen. And then it dawned on him. His son was recalling the experience from the day before and simply wanted to talk about it.

Was Garcia's belief based on reality or just wishful thinking? Was the baby actually initiating a conversation or was he just having fun with his hands? Who knows for sure but since the possibility does exist, why ignore it? If your baby makes a sign out of context, take the cue and start talking about airplanes or whatever else he's signing about.

You might try something like, "Yes, I remember those airplanes. Weren't they big and beautiful?" Then if you can, find a picture of an airplane to reinforce the idea and sign at the same time. At the very least these kinds of interactions help stimulate your baby's verbal language ability and will bring you closer together. And who knows, it could be step one toward your baby's talk show career.

The Least You Need to Know

- While they may not be your baby's favorites, DON'T TOUCH and GENTLE TOUCH are important signs to teach.

- When it comes to setting your goals, it's important to decide how proficient in sign language you want your child to become.

- To decide what additional signs you want to teach, pay close attention to your baby and see what he's interested in.

- Trust your instincts when it comes to adding new signs to your baby's vocabulary.

- While combining signs isn't essential, your baby may do so on his own to help clarify his message.

- When babies get to the stage when they are combining signs, they should also be speaking.

Chapter 6

Staying the Course

In This Chapter

- ◆ Learn how to stay motivated
- ◆ Incorporate sign language into your everyday routine
- ◆ Get help and support from family and friends
- ◆ Deal effectively with naysayers
- ◆ Stay on track with do's and don'ts

You've come a long way, baby. You, too, Mom and Dad. In fact, by the time you've reached this chapter there's not much left that I can teach you. You have a solid grasp of what's involved and what you have to do to make it happen.

My guess is that at this stage you feel one of two ways. You're either chomping at the bit and can't wait for your baby to reach the signing stage (if he's not already there), or you're a bit overwhelmed by it all and are having second thoughts about the whole thing. (Collective gasp!)

Rid yourself of all doubt! Of course you're going to do this! You're planning on teaching your baby to *talk*, aren't you? Well, teaching your baby to sign is just like teaching him to speak—except you're going to throw in a few visuals (signs) to add emphasis to what you're teaching.

Staying Motivated

What's the number one reason why babies don't sign? Their parents lost their motivation and stopped. Now I *will* admit that it does takes patience and commitment to teach sign language to your baby. And yes, it's true that you could go *months* waving your hands in the air without any reaction or feedback from your little one. But trust me when I tell you that *it will happen.*

So stop second-guessing yourself. If you've been following the guidelines, success is in your future. Don't compare your progress with anyone else's. Just think positively and move forward.

Uh-oh. That's it, isn't it? You talked to your cousin Shelley and heard all about how *her* baby signed at nine months. So now you think you must be doing everything wrong and that you're a total failure since *your* baby is a year old and nothing is happening. Ready for the pep talk?

You're not doing anything wrong, and you are far from being a failure! Do you know what you are? You're a wonderful parent who is doing a fantastic thing by giving your baby an extraordinary gift.

And why in the name of all that is holy are you listening to your cousin Shelley? You never liked her anyhow. Plus isn't she the one who's the lousy cook? Hey, that's it! Maybe her baby isn't signing at all! He could just be trying to cover his mouth so he doesn't have to eat her home-made baby food!

Okay, so what if her baby *is* signing? It has nothing to do with you. Your baby will sign, too—when he is ready. And when that day comes, all your efforts will have paid off big time and you'll wonder why you ever had the slightest inkling of a doubt.

Let me reiterate. Until your baby starts to sign, avoid asking other moms and dads about their baby's signing progress. Comparisons will only cause you needless concern. All babies have different developmental timetables and will crawl, walk, sign, and talk when they are ready.

So to those of you whose enthusiasm may be starting to wane, here's a sage piece of advice that my mother handed down to me. She learned it from her mother before her. Get over it! You've come too far to stop now. Just take a good look at your beautiful baby and think of what he'll miss out on if you do. Who, me, laying a guilt trip on you? No doubt about it. I'm shameless when it comes to this subject.

Take Note

The primary reason that babies don't learn to sign is that their parents give up. While signing may get repetitive until you first see results, push forward and keep your motivational level high. Boredom and complacency are hazardous to your baby's signing success!

Motivational Tips and Tactics

I have to be honest. Signing at first can be a bit repetitive. But keep in mind that it's only a short-term situation, one that will vanish the moment your baby makes his first sign. When that happens, you won't be able to stop yourself from grabbing your camera to record the moment for posterity. Your enthusiasm will be rekindled and you'll be proud of what you've accomplished, as you should be. So hang in there and keep your eyes on the prize. It's better than winning the lottery.

But while you're waiting for the big day, here are some tips that may help you keep the faith:

- ◆ Try focusing on the actual process of communicating with your baby and not just on the outcome. Appreciate the fact that you have such a wonderful treasure and be thankful for what he is doing *today*.

- ◆ Re-energize yourself by re-reading Chapter 2 on the benefits for you and your baby.

- ◆ Don't think of this as an educational exercise. Think of it as entertainment or as a challenge. Whatever works to keep you going.

- ◆ Ignore other people's comments about why it's not working, what you're doing wrong, or how they were more successful.

- ◆ Don't start too early. If you just brought your baby home from the hospital, you have about a seven-month wait before you should even begin. Start signing when you're likely to get more immediate feedback.

◆ Keep signing in the same situations. Once it gets to be habitual, you may not even realize you're signing until one day, when you least expect it, those little hands will start flying. And so will you.

◆ Share your experiences and frustrations with others in the same boat. There are online support groups for parents who are at various stages in the signing process (see Appendix C). Some parents have just started or are about to. Others are "old timers," having been at it for months! Join in the experience and ask a question, share your thoughts and know-how, brag about your baby, and have a laugh with parents from all over the world. But remember, no two babies are alike, and hard as it might be, use their success stories as inspirations—not as comparisons!

Finding the Time for All of This

If one of the reasons you're feeling a bit uneasy has to do with time constraints, perhaps my response to an e-mail from an overworked mom in Colorado will help:

Dear KinderSigns:

Thanks for all your hard work in helping us learn how to sign with our baby. I have read everything and you made it all very clear. The problem is that I don't think I can find the time to do it. We have two older children and they need our attention, too. Plus I have volunteer work and my husband travels quite a bit. And learning an entire sign language? Well, I just wish we had the time.

Signed,

Disappointed in Denver

Dear Disappointed:

Hey, Denver! Join the club! You are certainly not alone. Everyone's busy. We're all overscheduled with play dates, soccer games, cooking, cleaning, and maybe even trying to keep up with a career, but that's still no excuse. You're looking for a pass? Well, you're not gonna get one from me. I know I sound harsh and unsympathetic but this is far too important for you to abandon!

Plus who said you had to learn an entire sign language? You said that my instructions were clear? Apparently not clear enough. Here are some things you need to think about, girlfriend:

1. No one expects you to be a sign language expert. You only need to know a few basic signs.

2. You can teach as few or as many signs as you want. The number of signs you teach is not nearly as critical as the quality of the interactions you have with your baby.

3. Even if you just teach a few basic signs, your baby will benefit. If you find the time to teach him more, go for it.

4. Of course you shouldn't ignore your older children. Get them involved in this, too. They will love it!

5. Please know that you don't have to turn your world upside down in order to be successful. Work signing into your everyday routine. Do what you can. You'll find that it's easier than you thought.

I hope that helps. Write back if you need another dose of my motivational medicine. Good luck!

Diane Ryan

Cheerleader in Charge

> **Behind the Signs**
>
> While baby sign language has taken the world by storm, it's most popular in the United States and England. Check out the list of support groups in Appendix C. They are great resources to ask questions, share the excitement, and maintain your commitment. Plus you may meet someone from the other side of the world!

A Day in the Life of Baby Signing Parents

If you're in need of a personal time-management coach, consider the job filled. While I can't offer one-on-one consultation, let me try to help you with some examples.

Wondering how you can integrate baby sign language with your own real world? Let's join the Jones family and see how they're managing it:

> 7:00 A.M. Baby's up! Everyone's up! Time to head for the nursery and watch little Belinda's face light up when she sees you. It's also time for her DIAPER CHANGE followed by the question she's been waiting to hear, "Are you hungry? Ready to EAT?"

7:15 A.M. Whew! She really *was* hungry. Look at that empty bowl. ALL GONE. But maybe she wants MORE?

7:30 A.M. Hey, look who's making an entrance. It's DADDY! I LOVE YOU too, DAD!

8:00 A.M. Time to get dressed. Those new SHOES fit perfectly. And what cool SOCKS! Hey, where are you going with my HAT, DOGGIE?

8:15 A.M. Early appointment with the pediatrician. Belinda sure hates needles but she loves to ride in that CAR.

10:00 A.M. Snack time. CRACKERS, JUICE, and MORE of both.

10:30 A.M. A stop in the park on the way home to see the FLOW-ERS and BIRDS.

12:00 P.M. Lunchtime! EAT. MORE. MILK. BANANA. ALL GONE.

12:30 P.M. There's that lazy cat. GENTLE TOUCH.

1:00 P.M. SLEEP time.

2:30 P.M. TELEPHONE. Want to talk to GRANDMA?

3:00 P.M. Belinda's first step! Look who's walking! Look who's falling. Whoops! Sorry you're HURT/PAIN.

5:00 P.M. Time to make dinner. DON'T TOUCH the stove. It's HOT!

7:00 P.M. BOOK time. BATH time. TOOTHBRUSH time.

7:30 P.M. SLEEP time.

Do you get the idea? When you sign with your baby just do what you would normally do and sign whenever it makes sense. Do what you can, as much as you can, and as often as you can, and you will get positive results.

But What If I Work Outside the Home?

Sure, that all sounds great, for a stay-at-home parent, you say, but I have a full-time career!

The question: is it even possible to teach a baby to sign when so much time is spent away from him?

The answer: yes, it certainly *is* possible. Regardless of how many hours in the day you are away from your baby, you can still give him the gift of signing. You simply need to have a plan:

1. Make a list of all the caretakers in your baby's life. Do you have a nanny? Does a relative watch him? Do you take your child to a daycare center or pre-school? Write their names down.

2. Start thinking about how you will educate and update everyone on that list. Make sure your strategy includes a regular method for them to update you on your child's signing progress and vice versa.

3. If your child is about to enter a daycare center or pre-school, find one that is signer-friendly. There are many daycare centers and pre-schools that incorporate sign language into their curriculum. That's the ideal situation.

   If not, why not get proactive? More and more daycare centers and childcare facilities are looking for ways to enrich their teachers' training and incorporate new practices to benefit their "students." Call on a few and get their reaction. There are many parents on the same quest as you are. Plus childcare is a more productive and less stressful experience for teachers when they have a signing "clientele."

4. If you can't find a situation that's signer-friendly, then you need to revert to Plan B:

   - Let your sitter/childcare teacher know from the very beginning that you are signing with your baby.

   - Demonstrate the signs your baby is likely to use.

   - Bring along a sign language book or something similar that you can leave each day for reference.

Behind the Signs

Because parents are demanding it, an increasing number of day care and childcare facilities are adding sign language to their curriculum. In addition to it being a great marketing tool, teachers are finding that their "students" are better behaved. See Appendix C for training opportunities for childcare providers.

♦ Let your caregiver know which signs you're working on and ask her to be on the lookout for them. Ask for a daily verbal progress report.

♦ Keep the lines of communication open between you and your child's caregiver. Invite questions and promote a dialog at every opportunity.

5. When you bring you baby home from daycare, sign as much as you can in whatever situations are natural and appropriate.

You *can* teach your baby to sign even if you're not with your baby 24/7. Will it take longer to see results? Perhaps. But with more people signing in more situations, it could even speed things up.

Initiate the Draft!

Regardless of whether you work in or outside the home, there's another valuable resource that you should tap into to help achieve signing success. No matter what your situation, call for reinforcements!

SELECTIVE SERVICE NOTIFICATION

To: *Grandma and Grandpa Jones*
       Grandma and Grandpa Smith
       Big Sister Suzie
       Big Brother Brucie
       Brenda the Babysitter

You are hereby invited to convene at 2015 hours at the Mess Hall at 4124 Spruce Street to receive further instructions pursuant to your role in Operation: Baby Sign Language.

As loyal members of this company, we appreciate your ongoing commitment and dedication during previous missions and anticipate that same level of enthusiasm in assisting our smallest recruit.

John and Sally Jones, Co-Commanders

Headquarters Company

Why go it alone? Recruit the family for this major offensive. Not only will it make the process easier, it'll make it much more fun. Remember the old adage about many *hands* making lighter work. It takes on a literal meaning in this case.

Because your baby will benefit from many role models, recruit as many as you possibly can:

◆ **Grandparents.** If you are lucky enough to have grandparents nearby, their involvement is critical. Chances are they never signed to you as a baby and may think the idea a bit off the wall. This means that before you teach them the signs that your baby is making, you may need to convert them to the idea. Let them borrow this book or sit down with them apart from the rest of the family for a little one-on-one. Hopefully, your enthusiasm will be contagious.

◆ **Big brothers and sisters.** Be sure to include older siblings in the action. They'll love the attention that they'll receive and will feel special teaching their little sibling something of real value.

◆ **Babysitters.** Since it's often difficult, if not impossible, to find a regular sitter, have new sitters arrive early on their first assignment so you can explain what you're doing and the importance of their role in it. The Baby Sign Language Journal that you'll find in Appendix D is a great resource for new sitters in interpreting what your baby may be trying to "say." Of course, don't just hand them the journal as you walk out the door. Demonstrate the signs yourself, leaving the journal for reference and reinforcement.

It's a good idea to educate everyone right from the beginning, if at all possible, before your baby is ready to start to sign. Encourage all recruits to read this book or at the very least have a general understanding of the process, and make sure they know what your goals are and keep them up to date on your baby's progress.

If you get new recruits after the mission has begun, bring them up to date right away. Make certain that they know the signs that your baby is currently making—plus the ones that he hasn't caught onto yet. You never know who will be the first one to spot a new sign!

One final piece of advice about getting family members involved: I used the "initiating the draft" comparison because I thought it was a catchy way of getting the point across. But as you already know, no one is going to be motivated to join the effort if you act like a drill sergeant making demands and not allowing questions.

Smart Signs

Place a copy of the Baby Sign Language Journal on the refrigerator or some other conspicuous place. By keeping it updated with your baby's progress, all family members and babysitters will know exactly what's going on.

The best "recruits" understand the mission and know how important their own role is in achieving it. So when you do have that family meeting, think of it as a fun family project, something that you all can get involved in while doing something important for the littlest soldier. So, go easy. You can't afford for anyone to go AWOL.

Dealing With Naysayers

One thing that can really sabotage your efforts is people telling you that the whole idea of signing with a hearing baby is ridiculous. Others may say it's impossible, unnecessary, or even harmful. You know the type:

♦ "But, Joanne. I never signed with my baby. I just knew instinctively what little Bruno wanted. Maybe we were just closer to our babies in those days ...."

♦ "Look, it's only logical. You give your baby another way to communicate and you're going to be raising a mime. Might as well rename him Marcel Marceau."

♦ "Your baby has perfectly good hearing. Why treat him like he has some kind of disability?"

When you encounter people with attitudes such as these, you can either ignore them or try to convert them by sharing the research and the important benefits of signing. You might even loan them this book or give them a copy of their very own. How much energy you put into converting the ignorant or misinformed depends on how important they are to you and whether or not they have the potential to help you reach your signing goals.

You do need to realize, however, that some people are never going to open their minds to progress or change. You might talk 'til you're blue in the face and just won't win. If that happens, move on. You have other more important things to do—like signing with your baby. Don't waste your time listening to negative thinkers. They'll only sap your energy and enthusiasm. And who knows? Once they see how much fun everyone is having and see how responsive your baby is to the idea, maybe they'll see the light.

Take Note

Don't let negative thinkers get in the way of progress. While it would be helpful to get support from the in-laws, for example, if you can't convince them, move on without them.

Do's, Don'ts, and Don't-Even-Think-About-Its

Now all that you need to do is—stay on track. You have all the tools and knowledge that you need and your motivational level is high. But before I send you out there, let's review the key points you need to remember.

DO ...

◆ Speak as you sign.

◆ Sign only in context.

◆ Incorporate signs into your everyday routine.

◆ Repeat the signs you have taught.

◆ Get the family and other caregivers involved.

◆ Add new signs as your baby is ready.

◆ Use body language and real-life opportunities to reinforce what you've taught.

◆ Praise your baby for his efforts.

◆ Enjoy the experience!

DON'T ...

 ◆ Listen to skeptics and naysayers.

 ◆ Expect too much too soon.

 ◆ Show disappointment.

DON'T EVEN THINK ABOUT ...

 ◆ Quitting!

The Least You Need to Know

 ◆ The primary reason why babies stop signing is because their parents lost the motivation and quit.

 ◆ While signing may be repetitive at first, it's important to stay the course and keep your motivational level high.

 ◆ The best way to teach sign language to your baby is to incorporate signs into your daily routine.

 ◆ You can teach your baby to sign whether you are a stay-at-home parent or have a full-time career.

 ◆ For a more seamless signing experience, try to find a daycare center that already uses sign language in their everyday curriculum.

 ◆ Ask family members, babysitters, and friends to get involved.

Baby Sign Language Dictionary

Beginning Signs

Beginning signs are listed here in their order of importance. They should be introduced to your baby in this sequence. (See Chapter 4 for more.)

more

more

Bring the tips of your fingers together a few times.

eat

eat

Your hand moves back and forth to your mouth as if eating.

milk

milk

Your hand opens and closes as if you're milking a cow.

hurt/pain

hurt/pain

The tips of your index fingers touch.

help

help

Your palms are flat and tap your chest twice. (Adapted from ASL to make it easier for a baby to model.)

help #2

help #2

One hand lifts the other hand to represent the concept of "assistance." (Authentic ASL sign.)

diaper change

All fingers except your thumb fold to your palms. Bring your knuckles together and pivot in opposite directions. (This is the sign for CHANGE with "diaper" implied.)

diaper change

Snack Signs

apple

The knuckle of your index finger touches your cheek while your closed hand twists forward.

apple

banana

banana

One hand "peels" a banana, represented by an upright index finger.

bottle

bottle

Pretend to grip a bottle with one hand and place it on the palm of your other hand.

cookie

cookie

Your fingers make a circular motion as if using a cookie cutter on dough.

cracker

cracker

Tap your closed hand against your elbow.

drink

drink

Pretend you are holding a glass and taking a sip.

eat

eat

Your hand moves back and forth to your mouth as if eating.

finished/all gone

finished/all gone

Both palms face upward and then turn over and outward.

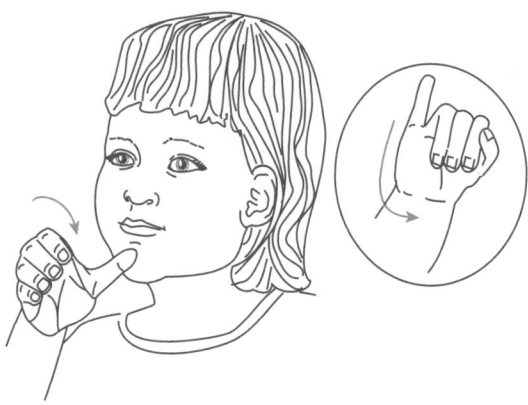

juice

juice

Make the sign for "drink" and then fingerspell "J," a downward hook made with your pinky.

milk

milk

Your hand opens and closes as if milking a cow.

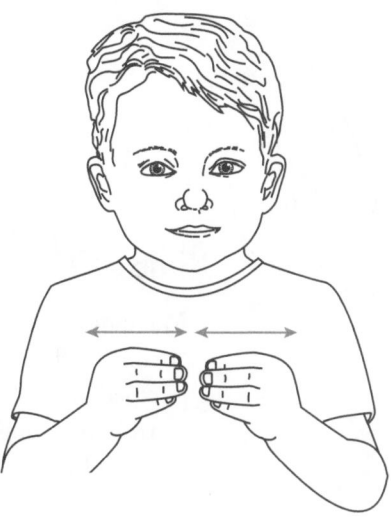

more

more

Bring the tips of your fingers together a few times.

water

water

Make a "W" with three fingers and place them at the corner of your mouth.

Good Manners

please

please

Your open hand makes a small circle over your chest.

sorry

sorry

Your closed hand makes a small circle over your chest.

thank you

thank you

Your fingertips touch your mouth and then move away from your body.

you're welcome

you're welcome

Your flat open hand moves outward from the front of your face to your waist.

Feelings and Emotions

angry

angry

Your fingers bend while pulling away from your face.

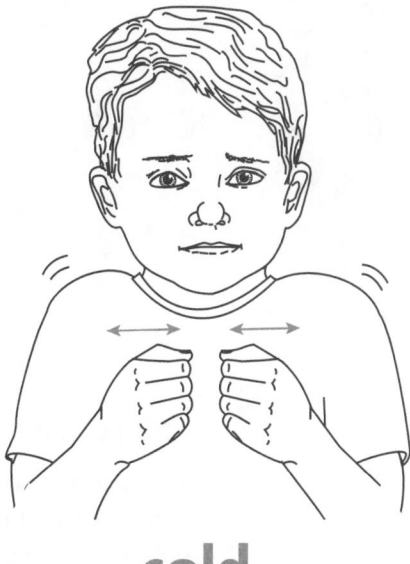

cold

cold

Your shoulders are
hunched forward.
Your hands shake as if
they were cold.

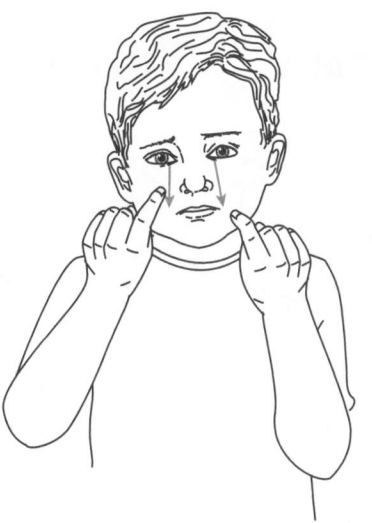

cry

cry

The index fingers of
both hands alternately
trace tears rolling
down your cheeks.

frightened

frightened

Your hand moves in front of your body as if you're trying to protect yourself.

happy

happy

Your hand moves upward on your chest indicating "high spirits."

help

help

One hand lifts the other hand to represent the concept of "assistance." (Authentic ASL sign.) Alternate: Flat palms tap your chest twice.

hurt/pain

hurt/pain

The tips of the index fingers touch.

i love you

i love you

Extend your pinky,
forefinger, and thumb.

love

love

Use both hands to
"hug" something over
your heart.

sad

sad

The fingers of both hands are outspread and move down your face to your mouth.

Behavior and Safety

bed

bed

Rest your tilted head on your hands.

clean

clean

One hand wipes "dirt" off the other one.

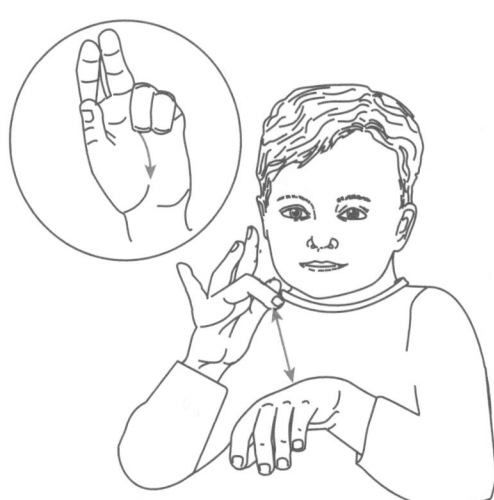

don't touch

don't touch

A combination of NO and TOUCH. The index and middle finger snap to the thumb indicating NO. Then the middle finger of the same hand taps the back of the other hand (TOUCH).

gentle touch

gentle touch

One hand gently "pets" the back of the other hand.

good

good

Your fingertips touch your lips and move slightly away from your mouth.

help

help

One hand lifts the other hand to represent the concept of "assistance." (Authentic ASL sign.) Alternate: flat palms tap your chest twice.

hot

hot

Your hand moves to your mouth as if you're about to eat. Then the open the hand moves away quickly as if it's too hot.

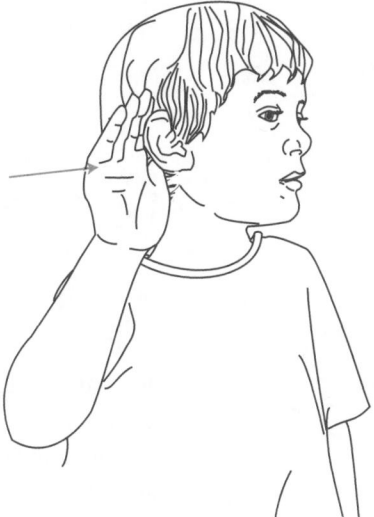

listen

listen

Cup your hand to
your ear.

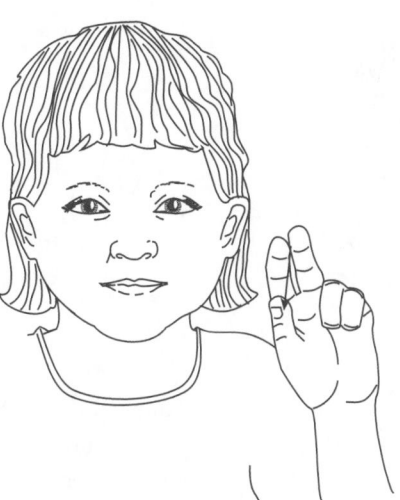

no

no

The index and middle
fingers snap to the
thumb.

quiet

quiet

The index fingers start at the mouth with one hand in front of the other. They then move downward in a silencing gesture.

sit

sit

The first two fingers of one hand "sit" on the same two fingers of the other hand.

share

share

One hand is held vertically with the thumb up. The other vertical hand slides back and forth over the index finger to convey slicing or dividing something.

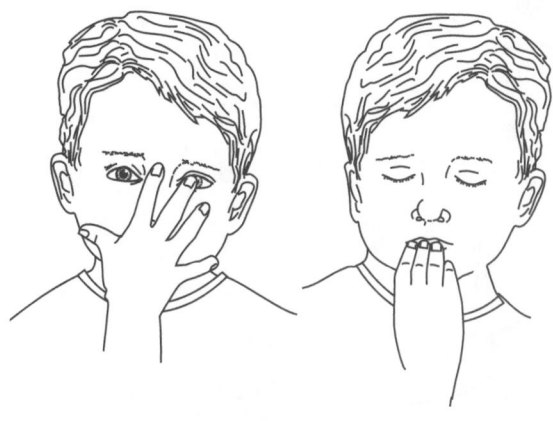

sleep

sleep

Your hand is held in front of your face. Your fingers are then drawn to your mouth.

slow

slow

One hand moves slowly up the back of the other.

speak

speak

Your index fingers alternately move back and forth from your mouth.

stop

stop

Your flat hand is held vertically and drops forcefully on your other hand.

wait

wait

Your palms are held upward up and your fingers wiggle. One hand is slightly in front of the other.

where

where

Wag your index finger back and forth.

yes

yes

Your closed fist moves up and down.

Games and Activities

ball

ball

Your hands are open
as if you're about to
catch a ball.

book

book

Your palms open and
close as if opening and
closing a book.

computer

computer

Your hand is shaped like a "C" and moves along your forearm.

dance

dance

Your index and middle fingers swing back and forth over the palm of the other hand.

fall

fall

Your fingers make a "V" and stand on your palm, then lie flat to indicate falling.

hide

hide

With your shoulders hunched, cup one hand over the other with the thumb peeking out.

jump

jump

Your fingers form a
downward "V" and
jump up and down
from your open palm.

music

music

Your hand moves
rhythmically back and
forth over your arm.

play

play

The thumbs and pinky fingers of both hands are extended and shake back and forth.

run

run

Each hand forms a loose "L" shape. The index finger of one hand pulls on the thumb of the other. As both hands move forward the index finger wiggles.

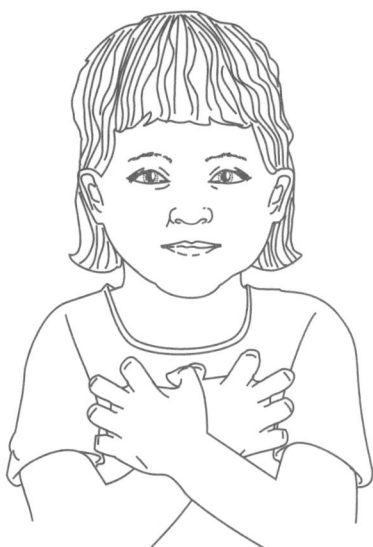

teddy bear

teddy bear

Your arms cross your chest and make a clawing motion. (Same as the sign for BEAR.)

telephone

telephone

Your thumb is at the ear and your pinky at your mouth.

Clothing Signs

coat

coat

Bring both arms forward as if putting on a coat.

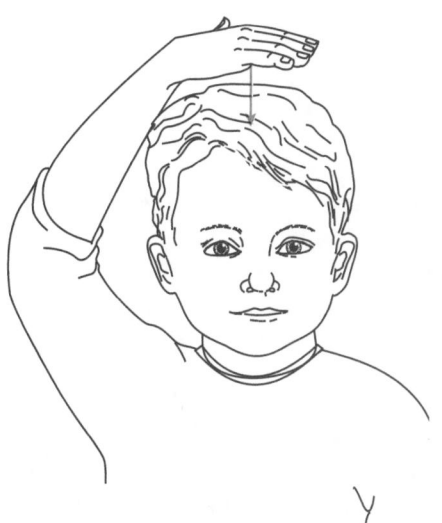

hat

hat

Your open hand pats the top of your head.

shoes

shoes

Tap your two down-ward fists together twice.

socks

socks

Both index fingers point down. One moves up and the other down, brushing against each other.

Family Members

mommy

mommy

The thumb of your open hand taps your chin twice.

daddy

daddy

The thumb of your open hand taps your forehead twice.

grandmother

grandmother

The thumb of your open hand taps your chin twice and then makes two arcs down and away.

grandfather

grandfather

The thumb of your open hand taps your forehead twice and then makes two arcs down and away.

sister

sister

One hand forms an "L" with the thumb touching the chin. It then moves downward to meet the other L-shaped hand.

brother

brother

One hand forms an "L" with the thumb touching the forehead. It then moves down-ward to meet the other L-shaped hand.

baby

baby

One arm cradles the other and both move side to side in a rocking motion.

Fostering Independence

down

down

Your index finger points downward.

help

One hand lifts the other hand to represent the concept of "assistance." (Authentic ASL sign.) Alternate: Flat palms tap your chest twice.

help

mine

Bring your open hand to your chest to signify ownership.

mine

more

more

Bring the tips of your fingers together a few times.

stop

stop

Your flat hand is held vertically and drops forcefully on your other hand.

toilet/potty

toilet/potty

Your index finger folds
over your thumb.
With the thumb peek-
ing out, shake your fist
back and forth.

up

up

Your index finger
points upward.

wait

Your palms are held upward up and your fingers wiggle. One hand is slightly in front of the other.

wait

want

Both hands are extended and then brought toward the body while the fingers curl up.

want

where

where

Wag your index finger back and forth.

yours

yours

An open hand moves toward the person you're addressing.

Outdoor Signs

airplane

airplane

Extend your index finger, pinky, and thumb. Move your hand to simulate flight.

bee

bee

Your index finger and thumb touch your upper lip and then brush across it as if brushing away a bee.

bird

bird

The index finger and thumb open and close at the lips.

butterfly

butterfly

Your thumbs lock and fingers flutter to look like a butterfly.

car

car

Hold your hands as if you were gripping the steering wheel of a car.

clouds

clouds

Shape both hands like clouds.

flower

flower

Draw your hand under
your nose as if sniffing
a flower.

grass

grass

Move your fingers
toward your mouth
with your thumb out
to simulate an animal
eating grass.

outside

outside

One hand comes out
of a opening created
by the other hand.

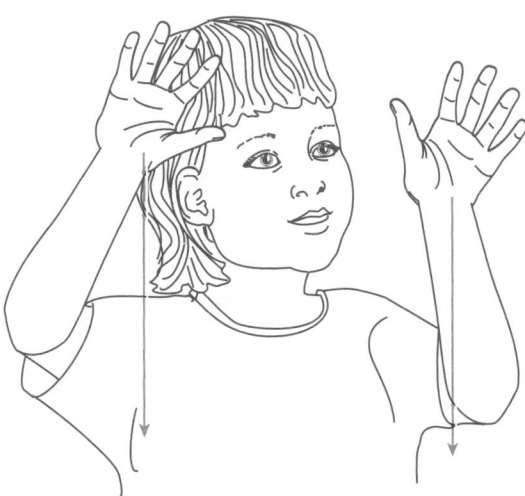

rain

rain

Your fingers are spread
and fall downward at a
slight angle to look
like rain.

sun

sun

Shape your hand like a "C" and look up at it.

tree

tree

Your arm is upright and supported by the back of your other hand. Your upright hand pivots from the wrist to represent a tree.

Animal Signs

alligator

alligator

Your hands open and
close like the mouth of
an alligator.

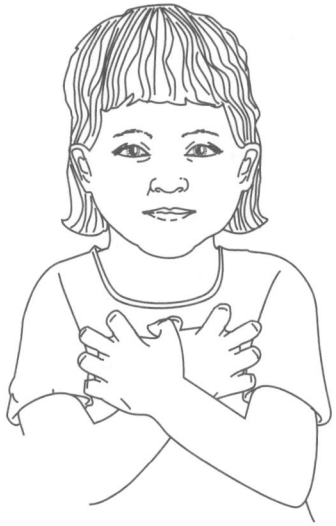

bear

bear

Your arms cross and
make a clawing
motion at your chest.
(Same as Teddy Bear.)

cat

cat

From the corner of
the mouth, your index
finger and thumb trace
a cat's whiskers.

cow

cow

Your "Y" shaped hand
looks like a cow horn
with the thumb touch-
ing your temple.

dog

dog

Snap your fingers
together. Alternate:
Slap your thigh.

elephant

elephant

Your hand is shaped
like "C" at your nose
and then slides down
the body like an ele-
phant's trunk.

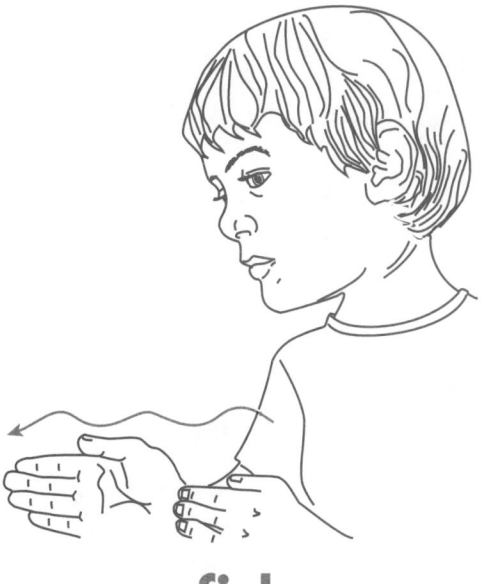

fish

fish

The fingertips of one hand touch the wrist of the other and mimic the tail of a fish.

frog

frog

Your index and middle fingers flick outward under your chin.

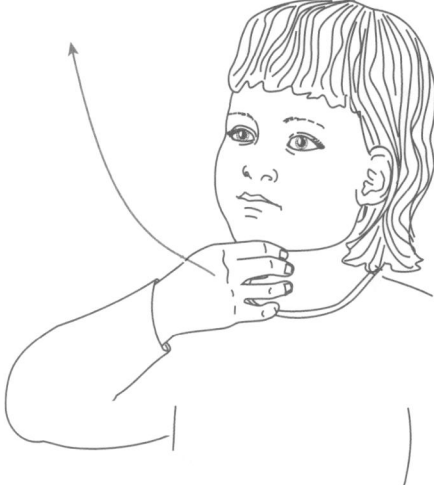

giraffe

giraffe

Your hand makes a grabbing motion at your neck and moves upward.

horse

horse

Two fingers wave like the ear of a horse while your thumb touches your head.

kangaroo

kangaroo

Your hands are held outward and jump forward to mimic the hopping motion of a kangaroo.

lion

lion

With your hand shaped like a claw, reach to the opposite side of your head. Then arc it back to simulate a lion's mane.

monkey

monkey

Your hands scratch your sides like a monkey.

rabbit

rabbit

With your hands facing backward, wiggle your index and middle fingers.

snake

Your index and middle fingers bend to simulate snake fangs and then move forward in several small arcs.

snake

spider

With your wrists crossed, link your pinky fingers and move your hands forward while wiggling your fingers.

spider

Good Grooming

bath

bath

Your closed hand makes separate circular motions as if bathing.

brush hair

brush hair

Your hand simulates brushing your hair.

brush teeth

brush teeth

Your hand mimics the
action of brushing
your teeth.

bubbles

bubbles

Your palms are face
down and your fingers
flutter upward.

mirror

mirror
Your hand is held as if it were a mirror.

shampoo

shampoo
Mimic the action of washing your hair.

wash

wash

Your closed downward hand circles your upward closed hand to simulate scrubbing.

wash face

wash face

Make the sign for WASH and then with your index finger circle your face.

wash hands

Make the sign for WASH and then the sign for HAND. Stroke the top of your hand with your fingers.

wash hands

Toilet Training

diaper change

All fingers except your thumb fold to your palms. Bring your knuckles together and pivot them in opposite directions. (This is the sign for CHANGE with "diaper" implied.)

diaper change

finished/all done

finished/all done

Both palms face toward you and then turn over and outward.

potty/toilet

potty/toilet

Your index finger folds over your thumb. With the thumb peeking out, shake your fist back and forth.

Part 3

The Transition to Speech

It's bound to happen. After all your hard work, the day will dawn when your baby realizes that the words he's learning are more important than the signs he's making. Isn't that gratitude for you?

Maybe for you, that day is already here. Of course, his first word was something that you looked forward to. But did it have to happen so soon? Why, it seems like only yesterday that he put those little fingers together and made his first *sign!* And now, he's starting to *talk!* Before you know it, he'll be in first grade and then dating!

But just because your baby is discovering new words, does he have to abandon the signs that have served him so well? Why quit now? Encourage your baby to continue the adventure as long as you can.

In Part 3, we'll take an in-depth look at what happens when speech enters the picture. In some ways it's like the onset of the "talkies" when the silent film stars were quiet no more. And you know the fuss *that* created.

Chapter 7

Look Who's Talking!

In This Chapter

- ◆ Learn about the long-term effects of signing
- ◆ Discover why and when babies stop using sign language
- ◆ Help your baby make the transition to speech
- ◆ Share "secret signs" with your baby
- ◆ Explore your options if your baby is a "late talker"
- ◆ Assessing sign language for children with special needs

Teaching your baby to sign was a memorable experience, wasn't it? But let's not dwell in the past tense. Even if you don't teach your baby any *new* signs, he'll still use the ones he knows for quite some time.

By the way, you should definitely give yourself one giant pat on the back. You have done a *masterful* job constructing the bridge from his pre-verbal days to his first words. But your baby has only taken a few tentative steps across the great divide. We need to get him all the way there.

Keep on Signing

When your baby starts to say a few words, don't stop signing to him. In fact, encouraging him to sign will help him make the transition to spoken language easier.

According to *Baby Signs* researchers Linda Acredolo and Susan Goodwyn, babies can benefit from sign language until they're *two-and-a-half years old*. They're still within that window of opportunity when their brains are primed for maximum stimulation in the language department. The longer you speak and sign with your baby, the brainier he'll become.

Think about that for a minute. If your baby said his first word at 12 months, for example, his brain will be positively impacted by sign language for another 18 months. And his brain will be *permanently* impacted by it throughout his entire life!

Why is that so? We've talked about it before but let's go over it again. It's important. Spoken information (your voice) is received and stored on the brain's left side. Visual information (signs) is stockpiled on the right side. Since sign language involves both audio and video, so to speak, more of the brain is stimulated. When your baby needs to search and recall information, he has two sources to tap into. The result? A smarter baby with a larger vocabulary who'll also have an easier time learning to read. And that doesn't even begin to address the *emotional* benefits!

My advice? Just keep signing, baby. Continue to reinforce the signs that your baby already knows and introduce new words and signs when opportunities present themselves. In other words, just keep doing what you've been doing. You're doing just fine.

Why He'd Rather Speak Than Sign

What will happen if you *stop* signing with your baby once he starts to speak? He will eventually drop his signs in favor of spoken words. Yes, he will have enjoyed the experience and benefited in so many ways—but his ultimate goal is speech. It's instinctive in all of us, after all. It's what we're programmed to do.

Like everything else, it will happen in stages. When your baby reaches a certain level in his development, the old way just won't be good enough any more. Especially not when there's a *better* way.

The day will come, if it hasn't already, when your baby will want a more sophisticated way to communicate. Yes, sign language will have helped him, but soon he'll need more than just a way to label things. While it still has a purpose—and may for some time to come—sign language will begin to lose some of its luster.

> **Smart Signs**
>
> Why would a baby use sign language when he can speak? One reason might be for emphasis, to make sure that he's really getting his point across. He may use DON'T TOUCH, for example, when you want to change his diaper. Or NO when you tell him it's time to go to bed. Yikes!

An Interview with a Baby-Signing Baby

Sometimes you get lucky. Just when I was racking my brain trying to think how I could best explain to you why a baby would choose speaking over signing, an expert dropped by who was willing to talk about it first-hand. I taped it for WCIG Radio so I could play it back for you. (That stands for *Complete Idiot's Guide*, in case you didn't figure it out.)

By the way, I agreed not to use his full name since his parents weren't aware of his "speech tendencies" and he wanted to open that closet door at a later date.

> D.R.: Hello and welcome to WCIG Radio. Our guest today is Bradley the Baby. A big welcome to you, little guy! Can you tell us a little bit about yourself?
>
> Bradley: Well, there's not much to say. My life is only beginning, you know. I'm just 13 months old.
>
> D.R.: But I understand that within that short time, you've become quite the little sign language expert.
>
> Bradley: You might say that. At first I was a little skeptical. I didn't really get what the hand signals were all about. But once I caught on, it made my life easier. Helped me get my point across. Less frustrated, you know. As you can see, I'm pretty relaxed.

D.R.: Why is it then that you're thinking of *quitting?*

Bradley: Take yesterday at the park, for example. There I was in the sandbox with two kids who I'd never met before. They were a little older and actually saying a few words. One little girl gave me a pail and shovel and I signed THANK YOU. They both looked at me like I was from Mars.

D.R.: So what did that tell you?

Bradley: That not *everyone* knows sign language! Those two kids were into something I didn't know much about. So I asked myself, "How are you gonna communicate with people who don't know what your signs mean?" So spoken language is something I'm looking into.

D.R.: Well, it sounds like you already have an incredible grasp of verbal language.

Bradley: This is really all make-believe, you know. I'm not actually talking. We're only doing this to make a point.

D.R.: And the point is that since there are people who don't understand sign language you'd better find a new way to communicate?

Bradley: Among other reasons.

D.R.: Such as …?

Bradley: It only works face-to-face. Yesterday I ran down the hall and signed MOMMY. I needed a DIAPER CHANGE. She was in the kitchen and couldn't see me. What good was sign language to me then? So I let out a howl and she came running. Sound is where my future is.

D.R.: Why, thank you Bradley. You've been most informative.

Bradley: One more thing. I'm a busy kid. There's a lot else to do with my hands. Eating, of course, but then there's finger paints, toys, and, rumor has it, a new trike in my future. I just can't drop everything to sign. I think it's time to move on.

D.R.: So you're abandoning your signs in favor of speech?

Bradley: Well, *abandon* might be too strong a word, but I'm definitely gonna scale back once I make a little more progress. When I get real good at it, hasta la vista, baby.

D.R.: Out of the mouths of babes. Our guest today has been Bradley. Signing today—speaking tomorrow. And now a word from our sponsor ....

Whew! That little Bradley is really something, isn't he? Precocious little guy, but he makes a lot of sense and speaks for many kids his age when he tells us why he'll stop signing:

1. Not everyone understands sign language.

2. Sign language only works face-to-face.

3. Babies have more interesting things to do with their hands.

How It Will All Play Out

Your baby's signs won't disappear overnight. Most babies use them well after they've begun to talk and will keep them as long as they're useful. That's important to remember. As long as a sign helps a baby or holds some interest for him, he'll continue to use it. But that also means that while you may continue to reinforce his old signs or try to teach him new ones, if the signs aren't relevant or meaningful to *him*, you're wasting your time.

Why would a sign be useful to a baby when he's learning to talk? Well, maybe the word that he wants to articulate is multi-syllabic. Try saying that sentence when you're 13 months old! Or perhaps he's just tired and he doesn't want to bother. Think of the reasons *you* use sign language. You don't sign? Maybe you don't use American Sign Language, but *you do sign*.

♦ You use signs for emphasis. "STOP right there and take off those muddy boots before you come in the house." It's much more effective when you hold your palm out in front of you, isn't it?

♦ What about when words just won't cut it? "I swear to you, the fish I caught was THIS big."

♦ When you take a giant bite out of a bagel with cream cheese and in comes Bobby. "Hey, Ma! Where's my ball cap?" If you know where it is, you point to it. If you don't, you shrug your shoulders.

◆ When you spot a friend across a crowded room and want her to TELEPHONE you later. Thumb to your ear; pinky to your mouth. (That *is* an American Sign Language sign, by the way.)

Behind the Signs

Based on our instinctive ability to understand facial expressions, body language, and generic signs, a Japanese company has received a technology patent that would enable your car to convey feelings and emotions to drivers around you. That means that instead of honking and flashing your lights, your car would get his (and your) point across by crying, smiling, or grimacing. It would also eliminate the need for the universal sign of disapproval that many drivers use to critique the driving skills of others.

Your baby will continue to use signs for those very same reasons. For emphasis, clarification, and maybe for a while, out of habit. When will he stop? It's hard to say. The crystal ball didn't work when you asked me when your baby would *start* to sign and it won't work now either. As before, there are too many variables.

Regardless of when the transition to speech does occur, it almost always happens in stages. Of course there are exceptions. There always are when it comes to a baby's behavior. But, generally speaking, here's what you can expect:

◆ Your baby will sign on his own without prompting.

◆ He'll say (or attempt to say) the word along with the sign.

◆ He'll drop most signs and keep a few favorites for clarification or emphasis.

◆ Words will take over and he'll drop the signs altogether.

You should be aware that at some point during the transition, your baby may have *two separate vocabularies*, one comprised of signs and another of words. He may devote all his energy to building his speaking vocabulary and not be interested in learning any new signs. He may be perfectly happy with the ones that he already knows. If you'd like him to learn a few more, try again in a few weeks.

On the other hand, he may be the type who just can't get enough. He wants to have it all. If that's the case, he may be open to learning new words *and* new signs. You just can't predict. Follow the leader.

Taking Corrective Action

Making the move from signing to speech is a complicated process for your baby. In effect, what he's doing is trading in one set of symbols (signs) for another one (words). Give him room to experiment with what works and what doesn't. But be vigilant! The signs that he's making may be clues to what he's trying to say. They may help you to decipher his meaning.

At first, you should expect that your baby's signs will be more accurate than his words. After all, he's been signing much longer than he's been talking. Again, pay close attention to his sign and body language. When you can figure out what your baby is saying, it's less frustrating for everyone involved.

Here's another important tip. Do you recall when your baby was beginning to sign and wasn't able to make the signs accurately at first? But you applauded his attempts anyway, right? Then you reinforced each effort by saying the word and showing him the correct way to make the sign.

Do the same thing now. If your baby says "Bah" for bottle, for example, show him how pleased you are that he is trying to speak. Maybe he's also made the sign for BOTTLE along with "Bah" so you know for sure what he's trying to tell you.

Let him know that you understand by making the sign for BOTTLE yourself. Then say something like, "BOTTLE! Yes, of course you can have your BOTTLE." Make sure you carefully say the word the way it's supposed to be said. Don't mimic his attempt. He needs to hear it the correct way so he has something to shoot for.

You and Your Baby's Secret Signs

There's another reason why you and your baby may want to hold onto some signs, even well beyond the stage when he has the ability to speak clearly for himself. Some signs may be—or can become—personal ways to communicate with one another without letting the rest of the world in on it. Well, at least the ones who don't sign anyway.

Remember in Chapter 5 when you learned the sign for DON'T TOUCH? I mentioned that it could be a sign that you and your baby could use when he got a bit older. When you were in a public setting and you didn't want him to touch something fragile, you could show him the sign. Better than a public tongue lashing, don't you think?

Another suggestion is the sign for TOILET. When your take your toddler to the park, he may lose track of time and not think about going to the restroom until it is too late. Instead of embarrassing him in front of his little pals, occasionally flash the sign with an inquisitive look to ask him to think about using the facilities.

> **Take Note**
>
> While silence may be golden in the "secret signs" arena, it's the only time you should offer a sign without its verbal equivalent. Signing without speaking will result in your child becoming a sign language expert. But will that help him recite the Gettysburg address or deliver a soliloquy on Broadway?

Those are just two situations when it may pay to be silent. You'll discover some of your own. Maybe to remind him to say THANK YOU to Aunt Lucy for the sailor suit, as ridiculous as it might be. Or to ask him if he needs HELP with the bullies on the playground.

I received the following letter from one mom who talked about another special way to use a "secret sign." I found it to be especially touching and thought that you might enjoy it, too.

Dear Diane:

My daughter Kara and I had a wonderful experience learning to sign and our entire family got involved. As she got older and her spoken language improved, she started to drop the signs that she had learned. While it was kind of sad to see them go, we were happy to hear her say one new word after another.

But there was one sign that she didn't drop. It was a sign that our family used then and continues to use today. It's the sign for I LOVE YOU. We got in the habit of using it whenever we would say good-bye.

This morning Kara got on the bus to go to kindergarten. It was not a day that I was looking forward to, believe me. My baby was not a baby anymore! I went with her to the bus stop trying to hide my tears as I watched her get on. As the bus pulled away from the curb she bravely looked out the window at me, smiled and made our secret sign.

Thank you for giving us all such a memorable experience.

Jane G.

Dallas, TX

Dealing With Speech and Language Development Concerns

Very early on in the book, I told you *emphatically* that when you signed with your baby, you had *absolutely nothing* to worry about as far as his language development was concerned. I also stressed that signing would *promote* your baby's language ability and that, in no way, would it hinder it.

So why deal with the subject if there is no correlation between signing and delayed language? Because many parents are concerned about it. It's a topic that I'm often asked about. And because sometimes sign language can help children who actually do (for any number of reasons) have delayed language.

The words *speech* and *language* are often used interchangeably but they're not the same thing at all. *Language* is a system of communicating with one another using sounds, symbols, and words to express meanings, ideas, thoughts, and emotions. It's a set of rules that we all share so we can exchange information.

Behind the Signs

While there may be any number of reasons why children have speech and language problems, none are caused by their having learned sign language as babies. In fact, a growing number of speech pathologists are using signs to augment traditional therapy and stimulate verbal language development in older children.

Speech is a part of the language system. It's a mechanical process that results in the formation of sounds and words. Speech is one way that language is expressed. Writing and signing are the others.

It's possible that a child may just have a *speech problem*. That means that his speech tools (tongue, teeth, lips, etc.) are not in the right place when he's trying to make a certain sound. If there are enough "inaccurate placements," people may have trouble understanding him. Since children acquire different sounds at different times, it could just be something to wait out. If there are numerous errors and your child is starting to get really frustrated about not being understood, you may need the help of a speech professional.

Then there are *language problems*. Some children have *receptive* language difficulties and have trouble processing exactly what you're saying to them. Others have *expressive* language problems and can understand what you have to say but find giving the information back to you difficult.

The whole thing is pretty complicated. So what's a parent to do if you think there's a problem?

If you think your child isn't speaking when he should, not as much as he should, or if others have a hard time understanding him, consult the following timeline. Keep in mind that children speak and learn language at different rates so the timetable is broad. That means that if your child's behaviors don't match others of the same age, there may be no need to panic.

Speech and Language Development Timeline

Birth–3 months	Makes pleasure sounds (cooing).
	Cries differently for different needs.
3–6 months	Increased interest in sounds and voices.
	Responds to changes in your voice.
	Makes gurgling sounds.
	Babbling sounds more like speech and includes different sounds including *p*, *b*, and *m*.
6–9 months	Turns and looks in the direction of sounds.
	Understands that vocalizations get attention.
	Understands his first words.
	Can imitate gestures and manipulate objects.

9–12 months	Begins to understand simple instructions like "Wave bye-bye."
	Understands approximately 12 words by 12 months (names of family members, pets, body parts, basic clothing, etc.).
	May say his first word. Most babies speak their first words between 10 and 15 months. The average is 12 months.
	Recognizes words for common items like *cup*, *shoe*, and *juice*.
	Begins to respond to requests ("Come here," "Want more?")
	Uses speech and noncrying sounds to get and keep attention.
	Imitates different speech sounds.
	Has one or two spoken words ("bye-bye," "dada," "mama") although they may not be clear.
12–24 months	Receptive vocabulary increases to as many as 300 words.
	Spoken language increases to an average of 200 to 275 words.
	Points to body parts when asked.
	Follows simple commands.
	Points to pictures in books.
	Says more words every month.
	Asks two-word questions ("go bye-bye?").
	Puts two words together ("more juice").
24–36 months	Vocabulary continues to grow.
	Ask "why" questions.
	Uses "no" and "not."
	Enjoys naming objects in picture books.

Source: The U.S. Department of Education

Behind the Signs

Albert Einstein didn't speak until he was three or four years old. (No one knows for sure. His mother didn't keep a baby book, apparently.) He didn't read until he was seven and also had trouble remembering his address. Pianist Arthur Rubinstein was also a late-talker.

The Late Talker Quiz

Still not sure whether your baby is developmentally on track? Then take the following "Late Talker Quiz" and see if there are any potential problem areas.

1. Does your 18-month-old say any words clearly?

2. Does your 20-month-old follow simple requests like "Come to Daddy?"

3. Does your 24-month-old put two words together like "More juice?"

4. Does your 2-year-old ask questions and respond to simple questions with "yes" or "no?"

5. Does your 3- or 4-year-old use language freely, experiment with verbal sounds, begin to use language to solve problems and learn concepts?

6. Do most people outside your family understand what your 3-year-old is saying?

Now ask yourself this final question: Do your instincts tell you that something is wrong? If the answer to this last question is "yes" and you answered "no" to any of the questions before it, then it's time to take the next step.

What to Do and When to Do It?

If you suspect that your child has a language delay, it is not caused by teaching him sign language. Often we don't know the reason why a child is a late talker. Rather than worry about what caused it, take action and get professional help to correct it. Talk to a pediatrician. Chances are, he or she will refer you to a speech and language pathologist (SLP) who will evaluate your child with special tests. A hearing test will also be included to rule out the possibility of related hearing problems.

Based on the test results, the SLP may suggest activities to do at home to stimulate development in this area. Often, that's all it takes. You may be advised to read more, use simpler words, and speak in shorter sentences to make imitation easier. You may also be encouraged to repeat what your child says, using correct grammar and pronunciation. This would allow you to demonstrate more accurate speech and language behaviors without directly correcting him. There are many different ways to tackle the problem.

Sometimes, the speech and language pathologist will look at the tests, the age of your child, and the extent of the delay, and recommend group or individual therapy. If your child is having difficulty being understood, sign language may also be recommended to reduce the frustration that can result.

Take Note

It is *critical* that a speech and language pathologist make the determination about teaching sign language to children with delayed speech. Don't assume that sign language will help your late-talking child and take it upon yourself to start. Without professional guidance, your child may learn that there is little or no need to speak when sign language works just fine. And that's something you don't want to happen, believe me.

It's important to remember that some children are just slow speakers and simply need a bit more prompting. Sign language may help as an interim way for them to express themselves while stimulating their verbal language. If used properly, these late-talkers may speak sooner than they otherwise might have.

Sign Language and Children with Special Needs

As you know, the focus of this book is to help pre-verbal *hearing* babies communicate with their parents through sign language. While sign language is a wonderful gift to give a child, a hearing baby will eventually learn to communicate without it. In other words, parents of hearing babies use sign language to enhance communication, not establish it. If you are the parent of a deaf baby, a more comprehensive and serious method of addressing the special needs of your child is in order.

In addition to the deaf and hearing impaired, there are other special-needs children who may benefit from using sign language. Teachers and parents of children with Down Syndrome in particular have credited sign language with making a huge difference in the children's communication skills as well as reducing their frustration.

Like all other kids, children with Down Syndrome develop at different rates but, in general, all learn and develop more slowly than the norm. Low muscle tone and difficulty with tongue mobility affect speech production and can make speech difficult to understand. Add to that the fact that these children have trouble recalling and organizing information, and you can understand the major communications problem that can result.

Recent studies in this area appear to offer a new direction. Basically they say that while Down Syndrome children have difficulty learning with their *ears*, they can do much better learning with their *eyes*. In other words, instead of teaching them auditorily, teachers are using more of a visual approach.

Behind the Signs

Down Syndrome is a genetic condition caused by extra genetic material from the twenty-first chromosome. It gets its name from the British doctor, John Langdon Down, who first clinically identified the condition in 1866. The actual chromosomal nature of Down Syndrome did not become documented until 1959 by Dr. Jerome Lejeune. However, Down's name remains associated with condition.

Using sign language with children with Down Syndrome capitalizes on their visual strengths rather than trying to improve upon their weaknesses. Children gain confidence and are less frustrated. Does verbal language take a back seat to sign language? Not at all. It's just another way of getting there. When children with Down Syndrome are taught visually, auditory weaknesses also strengthen and speech gradually improves.

While Down Syndrome has received the most "press" regarding its success with sign language, there are other disorders that may benefit from it as well:

◆ Children with *autism* may also find it useful as a way to communicate.

◆ Due to the inability to control muscles, some kids with *cerebral palsy* find that sign language facilitates communication.

◆ Children with *ADHD* (Attention Deficit Hyperactivity Disorder) also benefit from the use of sign language. When they use their hands to communicate, it occupies their minds and gives them the ability to stay on task. That in turn, enables them to better control their outbursts and interruptions.

Is sign language the ultimate solution or a panacea for children with special needs? Of course not. But it can be an effective tool. Parents and therapists who use sign language with special-needs children say it sure beats pointing and grunting. Since sign language is something that most children can learn easily, it also promotes positive situations that stimulate greater learning and often, improved speech and language skills. Plus sign language has the ability to decrease problem behaviors that may result when a child has trouble expressing himself.

The Least You Need to Know

◆ When babies learn that verbal language is more effective that sign language, they start to drop signs in favor of spoken words.

◆ Some babies continue to use signs to emphasize and clarify what they mean.

◆ Because children's brains are primed for language growth in the first three years, many parents continue to reinforce previous signs and introduce new ones after the onset of speech.

◆ Thee are some special signs that may serve you and your child beyond his early years and become "secret" ways for you to communicate.

◆ Children with delayed language may benefit from sign language but only under the guidance of a speech and language professional.

◆ Special-needs children, such as those with Down Syndrome, may benefit from sign language since it's been shown to stimulate verbal language development and reduce frustration.

Chapter 8

Promoting Your Baby's Verbal Language Development

In This Chapter

- ◆ Learn why your job has only just begun
- ◆ Discover ways to encourage your little chatterbox
- ◆ Understand the literacy and language connection
- ◆ Realize the lasting impact of what you've accomplished

What sets humans apart from every other species on Earth? We are the only ones that could come up with an advanced linguistic system to communicate with one another. We can't take personal credit, of course. We owe it all to evolution. But once our ancestors—and I'm talking *waaaay* back—figured out a way to express an infinite variety of distinct thoughts, we took one giant evolutionary leap away from whatever else was swimming in the sea, crawling on the ground, or swinging from the trees.

This amazing ability that we call *language* comes standard with all human packages. It's sort of like the SUV you just bought, except this feature wasn't fully loaded when it arrived from the factory. Plus there was no instruction manual that told you how to get from zero to three. (That's the window when your baby's brain is primed for maximum language growth.)

Okay, in plain English: even though your baby was born with the ability to communicate, that gift needs to be nurtured along the way. So far, so good. You've taught your baby to sign and now he's starting to talk. But now's not the time to rest on your laurels. There's a lot more to do! So if you're starting to clear off your desk thinking that the workday is over, punch that clock again—and put in for overtime.

Stan Spade, Speech Detective

Let's regroup for a minute and see what your baby's been up to. He learns so quickly these days, you really have to pay attention. In fact, monitoring his every move in the developmental department is so difficult that I took the liberty of putting a professional on the case. Meet Stan Spade, private detective. (I couldn't afford Sam, his infamous younger brother.)

It was a rainy night in the big city when I got a call from some speech pathology dame who wanted a stakeout on a certain subject. This was no one-night stand. She wanted the lowdown on this babe's every move for over a year. I checked out the subject and she was one sweet kid, real easy on the eyes. But I had to overlook that. After all, I'm a professional.

Her name was Samantha Smith, a 12-month-old cutie who didn't have much to say for herself. You know the type. A bundle of trouble wrapped up in a 22-pound package. Yeah, she'd say a few words here and there, but mainly got her point across with that smile of hers, and those signs she was using.

But then things started to happen. By 16 months she was coming on strong. There was no way this baby was ever gonna clam up. Maybe she didn't know what all the words meant at first—but this doll knew they were powerful. Had the men in her life wrapped around her little finger. Everybody else, too. She spoke, everyone jumped. She walked into a room, all eyes were on her.

And then things really started to pop. By the time she was two, she started making demands. No, she wasn't one to waste words. Mainly used two-word sentences like "More milk" and "Go out." Plus she threw in an occasional sign for emphasis until she got her way. They all do when they look like that.

Uh, nice job, Stan. I always did appreciate your flair for the dramatic, but this is costing me, so I'll take it from here. Ahem. By the time Samantha was three her vocabulary was rapidly increasing and she was starting to learn the rules ....

Rules? Babes like that don't like rules, sister.

Stan, you're off the case, remember? Besides, I'm talking about the rules of language. Rules we all need to know if we want people to understand us. Sorry for the interruption, readers. By age three Samantha was starting to develop a workable vocabulary but she needed a more sophisticated way to get her point across. She needed to learn about the rhythms of language, about grammatical structure and syntax ....

Can the lecture, sweetheart.

Your check's on the coffee table, Stan. Next to your fedora.

> **Behind the Signs**
>
> There are more than 2,700 languages in the world and 7,000 dialects all with different rules. The most difficult language to learn is Basque, which is spoken in northwestern Spain and southwestern France. It isn't related to any other language in the world and has an extremely complicated word structure and vocabulary.

Creating a Language-Rich Environment

While we were able to follow Samantha's behaviors in those early years, you'll notice that we didn't stake out the parents. But because Samantha made such excellent progress, let's assume that they did everything right during those critical three years and created optimal conditions to help her brain develop and mature.

What did they do exactly? They provided their daughter with a world that was *rich with sounds, sights, and consistent exposure to speech and language.* Plus while Samantha was unaware of it and even too young to take full advantage of it, her parents were in full accordance with the "Kids' Bill of Language Rights."

Take Note

Many parents think that "language development" is an automatic process. No so! There is nothing that any human being knows that he hasn't learned. This is especially true of language. So take heed, Mom and Dad, and do whatever is necessary to lay a proper foundation for your child's future language skills.

Truths, Apparently Not Self-Evident

On December 15, 1791, our forefathers formally added 10 amendments to the United States Constitution, known as the Bill of Rights. That much we all know. What wasn't as well publicized at the time was that the fore-*families* were all together in New York while this was going on.

While the fore-*mothers* were off shopping at some early version of Bloomingdale's, the fore-*kids* got together and created a "Kids' Bill of Language Rights." This was in direct response to the then-popular "children-should-be-seen-and-not-heard" school of thought.

While there is no solid evidence as to what actually occurred when the mini-bill was presented to the fore-*parents*, it is widely thought that the petitioners were given a big thumbs down and some quiet time in the stockade, a cruel and ironic punishment given the nature of their demands. Legend has it that one of the fore-*teens* managed to stash the document away for another try in a more enlightened era. Hopefully, that time is now.

The Kids' Bill of Language Rights

1. The right to start a conversation

2. The right to end a conversation

3 The right to speak uninterrupted

4. The right to ask questions

5. The right not to be ridiculed

6. The right to respectfully speak our piece

7. The right to set our own pace

8. The right to change topics of conversation

9. The right to be respected

10. The right to silence

By now you know me well enough to realize that I sometimes go to extremes to get my point across. So maybe there wasn't any "Kids' Bill of Language Rights." But even if you can't visit the original in some museum, its tenets should be etched in the hearts and minds of all parents who want their children to thrive. As your child's advocate and teacher, you can't afford to fail. Your mission (and you've no choice but to accept it) is to establish an environment that's conducive for expression and experimentation. You need to motivate, educate, stimulate, and sometimes, back off.

Tips from the Trenches

Now that you know what goes into creating an environment that's rich in language possibilities, it may be time to evaluate your own attitudes and surroundings. Or maybe you just need some inspiration on how to do it better.

Let's go right to the source. I've asked parents to share their ideas on what's worked for them and/or what they think is important in promoting their own baby's language skills. Some ideas may not apply to your child's age and developmental level. Others may be obvious to you and already part of your routine. But you may find an inspirational nugget or two to add to your own list of standard practices:

- ◆ "We've made it a family rule to respond in some way to every type of communication Emily makes, whether it's a sign or a spoken word."—Jones family, Brooklyn, NY

- ◆ "We make an effort to speak slowly, naturally, clearly, and in full sentences."—Pete and Kristen G., Durham, NC

- ◆ "Baby talk is not spoken here!"—Tim and Mary D., Amherst, NY

- ◆ "When Jeremy says a word incorrectly, we say the word the right way and never let anyone in the family make fun of his mistake." —Kelly and Mark M., Nashville, TN

◆ "We don't do anything fancy. We just encourage Alex to imitate our actions, including clapping hands, throwing kisses, and playing games like pat-a-cake, peek-a-boo, and itsy-bitsy-spider."—Matt and Kristin R., Grand Rapids, MI

◆ "I have in-depth conversations with Katherine, even if it's mostly one-sided. I explain to her what I'm doing and why. Then I ask her questions. I supply the answers, of course, but she seems to be taking it all in and trying to figure it all out."—Michelle R., New York, NY

◆ "I make sure to get together with other mothers for play dates. I think it's important that our toddler be exposed to all kinds of conversations."—Linda R., Boulder, CO

◆ "Silence can be a good thing sometimes. It gives a child time to think about what's been said and how he wants to reply."—The Brownings, Burbank, CA

◆ "We're always careful about asking Aidan too many questions at once. My husband works for the F.B.I. and we don't want our conversations with our baby to sound work-related!"—John and Melinda F., Reston, VA

> **Smart Signs**
>
> A language-rich environment doesn't mean a household where the TV is blasting and talk-radio playing constantly. Your baby's language will be enhanced only by direct human contact, conversations, and reading.

◆ "We just have fun identifying colors, teaching animal sounds, singing nursery rhymes, bouncing and dancing to the rhythm of music. And we sign, too, of course."—Gionelli family, Orlando, FL

And the number one suggestion from parent after parent ...

◆ "The best thing we do together is read."

The Language and Literacy Connection

Most dictionaries define "literacy" as the ability to read and write. Today the definition has been expanded. Many now consider it to be the ability to communicate using a wide range of resources including text, visual, audio, and video sources. For our purposes, we'll stick with the reading and writing components. But how does reading and writing promote your baby's language development?

Just as with language, literacy begins in the first three years of life. No, your baby won't start to read and write at this stage, but the synapses that will support those skills down the road are building. Remember in our earlier section when I said that babies who are taught sign language become better readers? So will the kids whose parents speak and read to them regularly.

A pre-verbal baby will first learn a few basic signs before moving on to verbal language. From there, the focus moves to writing. One thing helps another. In fact, the relationship among the three developmental areas is profound. When you nurture one area, all the others benefit from the extra attention.

Literacy is obviously linked to a child's experiences with books. So is language. When you read a book to your child, you're adding another building block to his language and literary development. Reading to him not only helps develop his language skills by increasing his exposure to it, it sparks his imagination and allows him to explore his feelings through the characters that he meets.

Let me sum it up this way. If you won the lottery and could afford to give your child anything in the entire world, I would tell you to put your money away. What your child needs, everyone can afford. Teach your baby to sign. Speak to him as often as possible. And read to him every day.

Take Note

Formal instruction that encourages babies and toddlers to actually read and write is not developmentally appropriate. Literacy skills should unfold naturally through books and positive interactions. Trying to teach a baby to read could even be counter-productive since children may begin to associate reading and books with failure.

Once Upon a Time

As you've seen, the importance of reading to your child is immeasurable. Not only does it stimulate thinking skills, imagination, and language development, it's a great way to spend quality time together.

Read to your child wherever and whenever you can. The doctor's office, a bench in the park, the bus, and the beach are all great external choices. At home, find a favorite reading area and get into the habit of reading every day. Then add some spark to the routine by having different family members read *with* your child. Did you notice the word that was just emphasized? You should read *with* your child, not *to* him.

Once upon a time reading was done in the style of Ward and June Cleaver of TV's *Leave It to Beaver*. If you're not old enough to have witnessed that unique parental approach, maybe you can catch it on the Nostalgia Channel:

Why, hello, Beaver. How was school today?

We didn't have school today, Dad. The teachers had a conference or something. I guess they needed to figure out new ways to be mean to us kids. I'm kinda bored.

Well, why don't you read a good book, Beaver?

Hey, Dad! I got a better idea! Maybe you could read one to me! Remember when I was a kid you read to me all the time? You let me turn the pages and ask questions. And we always looked at all the pictures. We used to wonder what the characters were like and drew their pictures after we finished the story. And when it was a sad book, you asked me how I felt about it. Like the time that Humpty Dumpty guy fell off the ....

Now, Beaver! I realize you're bored, but making up stories is never the right thing to do! I don't know where you get your ideas, Beaver, I really don't. There is no self-respecting 1950s TV father who would ever do what you've just described. Well, maybe Ozzie Nelson, but certainly not me. Why, I don't even remember reading to you at all! That was your mother's job. By the way, please ask her when dinner will be ready.

As a modern day parent you are, of course, more enlightened than Ward Cleaver. Why else would you be reading this book? You're looking for ways to maximize your child's every potential. Since reading is high on that list, it's something you need to take seriously. Sure, it's a wonderful part of your child's bedtime routine, but that's only the beginning. Books are great during the daytime, too! The more you read with your child, the broader his horizons and the greater his language potential.

By the way, if you're looking for tips to make reading a more interactive experience, I've added a few here, or you can re-read Beaver's plea to his dad. Sometimes fathers *don't* know best. (I know, different show.)

♦ As you read, ask questions about the story, the characters, and what might happen next, even if you have to supply the answers.

♦ Take time and describe the pictures on each page.

♦ See if your child can point out the shapes and pictures on the pages.

♦ Let him turn the pages.

♦ Ask your child to repeat words and phrases.

♦ When he's old enough, ask him to re-tell the story to you.

A Lifetime Legacy

In our next chapter, you'll graduate to the final step in our program and learn how sign language will benefit you and your *toddler*. Since there are distinct benefits specific to that age group, I urge you to move forward.

But I have to be realistic. I know for a fact that most parents don't sign after their child is around two years of age. They feel that they have maximized the benefits of signing and want to concentrate on speech and language development.

That means that many of you will be ending your sign language education here. But I refuse to say good-bye. I'm hoping that you'll return for a refresher course when you have a question or when your next baby comes along. By the way, you can send any questions on the subject to me at diane@kindersigns.com. I'd love to hear your success stories, too.

But if you are leaving me now (sniff), please know this. Regardless of how many signs you have taught your child, you have done something that is truly exceptional. When you combine the amount of time you've spent teaching your baby to sign with the care you've taken to enhance his verbal skills, it all adds up to an invaluable experience for both you and your child. You have given him an extraordinary gift.

Your child now knows that his thoughts really matter. He feels good about himself and has learned to trust others. He has discovered that learning is fun and worthwhile. He knows that he can rely on you and other family members and that you all love him. And that's a legacy that will last throughout his entire life. Job well done!

The Least You Need to Know

◆ Once your child starts to talk, you need to set the stage for additional progress and learning.

◆ Language and literacy skills begin in the first three years of life and are intricately connected.

◆ Of all the things you do for your child, reading with should be at the top of your list.

◆ When you teach your baby sign language and promote his verbal development, you have given him a legacy that lasts a lifetime.

Part 4

The Advanced Signer

Welcome to the advanced class! Some of you have been with me since the beginning and are now interested in continuing your baby's sign language education. To you, I say, "Well done, good and faithful student!" You've done an excellent job and I'm thrilled that you want to learn more.

Ah, but I see some *new* faces out there! You may be a little late to the party, but the important thing is that you're here now. Research has shown that children up to age three benefit from learning sign language. Plus at your child's "advanced age" things will go much faster.

By the way, you don't have to worry about make-up classes. I'll bring you up-to-date with some special assignments to help you catch up with the rest of the class and bring you up to speed.

So, if you have a toddler between 18 months and three years, you're in the right place. Ready to begin?

Chapter 9

Sign Language for Toddlers

In This Chapter

- ◆ Discover why it's a good idea to teach sign language to toddlers
- ◆ Learn a few tips before you get started
- ◆ Formulate a plan of action
- ◆ Stay on track with the "ten signing commandments"

Can I ask you a personal question? Why do you want to teach sign language to your toddler? Well, regardless of your reason, it's a good one. Maybe your child is already an expert and has been signing since he was a baby. Now he's demanding *more*! That's a great reason.

Or maybe your cousin, Shelley, told you about the wonderful experience she's had signing with her baby. Being motivated by others is also a good reason to start. The only problem is that cousin Shelley told you that it was too late to start signing with your 20-month-old. Nonsense! I'm glad you didn't take her word for it and came here to check it out for yourself.

Toddlers can benefit from signing until they're at least three—and maybe older. There's no need to worry about starting a bit late. We'll get you and your toddler up to signing speed in no time. And you can leave cousin Shelley in your dust.

Note: if you are starting your sign language education at this stage of the book, I suggest reading Chapters 1 and 2 and the section about "Your Baby's Amazing Brain" in Chapter 3. Better yet, read the entire book.

Why Bother?

Let's get a bit more specific about why it's a good—no, make that *great*—idea to teach a toddler to sign. Most of you already know the answer, I bet. Or at least you have a pretty good idea.

Like most parents, you've heard about the benefits that signing offers and want in on the action. Speaking of benefits, newcomers, did you check out the benefits for babies and parents in Chapter 2? That entire list of benefits is also yours when you sign with your toddler. No extra charge.

In case you'd rather read that chapter later, here's the jist: When you sign with a baby or toddler, you stimulate more of his brain and open the door to a host of other developmental extras. Signing helps to accelerate language development, builds larger vocabularies, and makes learning to read easier.

On the emotional side, a signing child is less frustrated, has a closer bond with his parents, feels good about himself, and is having one heck of a good time. Signing is, after all, *fun!*

There are major plusses for parents of toddlers, too. One will become especially near and dear to your heart. Studies have shown that one reason for the so-called "terrible twos" is a child's inability to express himself. That can lead to trouble.

Learning to talk doesn't happen overnight. While toddlers are soaking up information and showing off what they've learned, their language ability is still quite limited and things get in the way of progress. Sometimes a toddler gets tired or maybe he says a word but no one can decipher it. Why, that can really upset a kid—big time! What happens then? First he simmers, then he smolders, then he steams—and then he BLOWS!! Look out, TEMPER TANTRUM!

"Excuse me. But that's not always the case."

Why, if it isn't Bradley! Welcome back! For those of you who are just joining us and didn't meet Bradley in Chapter 7, you need to know that Bradley was invaluable in helping me explain why babies eventually stop signing in favor of speech. As you can see, he's just a baby himself.

"As a matter of fact, I'm a toddler now, 19 months to be exact."

And did you stop using sign language, Bradley? You said you were thinking of quitting?

"As I recall, I never used the word *quit*. I said that I was thinking about scaling back. But I've learned a few new signs since then and I keep of few of the old favorites in my back pocket for emergencies."

Emergencies?

"It's like you said. Sometimes I can't think of the word or no one's taught it to me. Why, sometimes my own mother doesn't understand me. But while I may not be able to get the word out, I sometimes *do* remember the sign. That really helps a lot. Reduces my frustration level. As you can see, I'm quite relaxed."

Yes, you mentioned that the last time, Bradley.

"Now that I'm a toddler, let's make that *Brad*."

Well, there you have it. That Bradley, uh, I mean, *Brad*, is quite the early-talker. It's obvious that his parents taught him to sign. And he's certainly not lacking in the self-esteem department. Another wonderful benefit of signing, of course.

Some Advice Before Getting Started

If you've been with me since the beginning of this book, you will have introduced the basic signs to your baby differently than we're about to demonstrate them here. No need to worry. Regardless of what you and your baby have done before, just follow the techniques that are presented. These alternate methods will reinforce what your baby already knows.

Here are a few tips to consider:

♦ Depending on your toddler's age, what you're about to learn may be more comprehensive than you need at first. Start slowly and move on to another lesson as you see fit.

Behind the Signs

You'll teach your toddler American Sign Language (ASL), the official language of the deaf community in the United States. ASL is completely separate from English and has its own rules for grammar, punctuation, and sentence order. But don't worry, we won't have to deal with any of that.

♦ Select signing categories that make sense to you and will interest your child.

♦ Customize the material to the age of your toddler and your own daily routine.

♦ Teach signs in whatever sequence works best for you.

Your Plan of Action

I know you're anxious to begin, but first you need a plan. Think everything through before you make that jump and find you're in over your head:

1. Decide exactly *when* you want to begin introducing signs to your toddler. Don't start until you're sure that you are ready. Once you begin, signing needs to be consistent.

2. Teach the Snack and Meal category first since it's the easiest and your child will catch on quickly. Good Manners would be the logical next step. You can take it from there.

3. Remember that it's not necessary to teach every sign in every category. Use whatever makes sense to you. Select the signs and categories that you want your child to learn and memorize them ahead of time. Taking it one category at a time will make it easier.

4. Rather than thinking of this as teaching *signs*, teach *associations*. Your child may be able to imitate your gestures, but he needs to know what they represent before he can use any of them meaningfully.

5. Meet with other family members for a practice session. Everyone must be familiar with the agreed-upon signs and ready to use them consistently.

6. Inform babysitters and teachers about the program and enlist their support. The more people who sign with your child the better.

7. Concentrate on one category for at least a week before moving on to another. Then move on to other categories at your discretion. Trust your instincts.

8. As with anything else that you teach, repetition and reinforcement are key.

9. Keep things simple, natural, relaxed, and by all means, enjoyable.

10. Obey the "ten signing commandments" that follow.

Take Note

Don't listen to anyone who says you can't go it alone! If you're a single parent or if other family members aren't interested, you can still teach your baby to sign. While a group effort might make things go faster, the most important success factors are dedication, consistency, and love.

The Ten Signing Commandments

Follow these do's and don'ts to keep you on the straight and narrow—and help you achieve signing success:

I. Always sign in context.

II. Once you begin to sign in a certain situation, continue.

III. Remember to speak as you sign.

IV. Use body language along with maximum facial and vocal expression.

V. Encourage a reluctant child to sign by occasionally (and gently) shaping his hands.

VI. Reward your child's efforts—even if just comes close and approximates a sign. Cheer him on!

VII. Use any and all creative ways to reinforce signs.

VIII. Never show disappointment or express any negative reactions.

IX. Have patience! Don't expect instant results.

X. Make the sign language experience meaningful and fun!

The Least You Need to Know

◆ One of the primary advantages of teaching a toddler to sign is to reduce the frustration that comes with not having the right words at his disposal or not being understood.

◆ Children can benefit from learning sign language until they're about three years old and maybe older.

◆ Before you begin to sign with your toddler, make sure you are ready with a plan of action.

◆ Achieve success by following the "ten signing commandments."

Chapter 10

Learning by Example

In This Chapter

- ◆ Learn the most common teaching categories for toddlers
- ◆ Follow step-by step instructions for the most popular signs
- ◆ Find out why teaching by example is the best strategy
- ◆ Enjoy tips and techniques in all signing categories

You and I have come a long way, baby! From the early days when we discussed the research and benefits of teaching sign language to your hearing baby to the time when you actually taught your little one to sign. It's hard to believe that now he's a toddler and ready for more.

I think congratulations are in order for both of us: for you, because you've already achieved signing success and are still moving forward; for me, because I got you here! But maybe I'm being a bit premature with all the kudos. You still need to motivate your toddler to learn some additional signs—and I've got to teach you how.

Teaching Categories

While there are many useful categories that you'll find in this book, I've selected the following for teaching purposes. The principles and techniques that you'll learn can be easily adapted to any of the other categories. Refer to the dictionary in the middle of the book to see how these signs are made.

> **Smart Signs**
>
> Illustrations and instructions for all signs are listed according to category at the middle of the book. For an animated demonstration of each sign and many more, visit the ASL sign language browser at the University of Michigan's Communication Technology Lab. They have generously given us permission to cite their incredible resource. Go to http://commtechlab. msu.edu/sites/aslweb/ browser.htm.

- ◆ Snack and Mealtime
- ◆ Good Manners
- ◆ Behavior and Safety
- ◆ Games and Activities
- ◆ Feelings and Emotions
- ◆ Animals
- ◆ Toilet Training

Snack and Mealtime

When you teach the signs in this category, you'll be using a two-level approach. In Level #1 you'll teach some generic signs that are associated with eating. Once your toddler gets the idea, you'll present him with specific labels for what he wants (or doesn't want) to eat.

Level #1:

EAT	MORE
DRINK	FINISHED/ALL DONE

Level #2:

APPLE	JUICE
BANANA	MILK
COOKIE	WATER
CRACKER	

Why is the Snack and Mealtime category the best place to begin teaching your toddler to sign? It's because snack and mealtime are already part of your everyday routine. That makes them perfect "educational" opportunities. When you teach the signs in this category, you'll simply be capitalizing on an already positive experience, one that your child likes and looks forward to. When your toddler knows a few related signs, he'll have something else to make snack and mealtime even more fun and interesting.

Take Note

Teaching in context takes on a whole new meaning in the snack and mealtime department. When you teach a certain food sign, the object will obviously be there to help make the association. Just be sure to stock up ahead of time and be prepared when your toddler finally makes the sign himself. If you're out of apples when he makes that sign, handing him a banana will set your efforts *waaay* back.

Tips and Techniques

1. There is no right or wrong way to teach a sign. Your goal is to simply develop a natural way for your toddler to associate the sign with the idea that you're trying to convey.

2. You can teach the signs in the order that you'll find here or in any other way that seems logical to you. After all, it has to fit in with *your* routine. Make sure that you learn all the signs in this category before you begin.

3. Introduce all Level #1 signs during one meal. Don't expect your child to remember them all right away, of course. While it may seem like a lot at first, think of it as a "signing showcase," a presentation of the signs that you want him to learn.

4. Make sure everyone is seated around a table where your child can see what's going on. Then demonstrate that it's time to EAT by showing the sign and taking a bite of something. Then ask another family member if he would like something to EAT. He responds that he would and says, "Yes, I would like something to EAT." He then demonstrates the sign and gets his "reward."

5. Then ask your child the same question. Example: "Bobby, would you like to EAT? I'm hungry. I think it's time to EAT." Every time you say the word, make the sign. Then reinforce it by either taking a bite of something or pretending to.

6. Introduce DRINK, saying and signing the word. Then take a drink of something. Have another family member do the same. Ask others if they would like a DRINK. They respond by signing and stressing the word. Repeat this a few times.

7. The next sign is MORE. Ask/sign if anyone would like MORE of something. When a family member responds that he would like MORE by using the sign, make sure he receives something.

8. To bring this lesson home to your child, give him one Cheerio and ask/sign if he would like MORE. Before he can get upset, give him another. Then repeat. This will help him to make the association. Make a game of this. Be happy. Smile!

9. Decide on which word(s) you will use (FINISHED or ALL DONE) and stick with it. When your toddler is finished, ask if he is ALL DONE. Do that a few times. Ask others if they are ALL DONE and they respond by making the sign before handing their empty plate to you.

10. Ignore the fact that this will seem awkward at first. What I have given you is the "shell" of the session. You need to add your own personality. By the way, you don't have to memorize your lines. (I hope you knew that!) Those were just ideas to get the idea across. In between each signing demonstration, act normally. Laugh and talk about other things. Once in awhile when the time is right, add a signing demonstration. This has got to be fun for everyone.

11. Once you start signing during Snack and Mealtime, continue to do so. With enough repetition your family will feel more comfortable with the idea and your toddler will catch on quickly.

12. When you feel your toddler has a good grasp of the more generic concepts in Level #1, it's time to graduate to the next step and teach signs that are related to specific items. But remember not to abandon the signs you have already taught. Continue to use them whenever appropriate.

13. Teach the signs in Level #2 the same way. Show a BANANA, for example—make the sign and say the word. A day later, try the sign for JUICE. Repeat them often enough and your child will catch on. One day when you least expect it, he'll look at you and make the sign on his own. Make sure you have lots of everything handy. You don't want him to think that he's signing for no reason.

14. Introduce the other signs whenever you like. The important thing to remember is that you need to continue using the signs if you want your child to learn them.

 **Smart Signs**

By 18 months your toddler should be speaking, or at the very least attempting to say words. Because your goal is to get him to sign *and* speak, never sign without saying the word. And don't anticipate your toddler's every need. Encourage him to sign and ask for what he wants.

Good Manners

PLEASE   THANK YOU

SORRY   YOU'RE WELCOME

The Good Manners category is the next logical step after Snack and Mealtime signs. Regardless of whether they're spoken or signed, these concepts are difficult for a child to understand. We say PLEASE as part of a request for something, and THANK YOU when we get what we asked for. Then the person who gave us whatever we requested responds by saying YOU'RE WELCOME. Will this personally benefit your toddler? Maybe not at the moment. Just think of it as an early introduction to the rules of proper etiquette.

Tips and Techniques

1. Again, this has to be fun. A toddler's primary motivation for learning these words and signs is to "please" you! Since there are no concrete associations for your child to make, he'll learn through habit. But he won't be motivated at all unless you make it enjoyable.

2. The best way to teach PLEASE and THANK YOU is to not make a big deal out of it. You are going to teach these signs by example.

3. While your child is at the dinner table with you, ask another family member for something—but use *lots* more spoken emphasis than you would normally. Then exaggerate the sign itself. Example: "Suzie, may I PLEASE have a napkin?"

4. When you receive what you asked for, exaggerate THANK YOU as you sign and smile.

5. Suzie's job isn't over. She now has to dramatically say and sign YOU'RE WELCOME.

6. Continue this strategy for a few days before you encourage your child to try it himself. Encouraging him by gently taking his hand and guiding it through the signing motion. Only do this occasionally as a way to motivate him—but *never* force him to sign.

7. Results will depend on the age of your toddler and how often and consistently you sign with him. He may pick up the idea immediately or it could take a few weeks. Stick with it, though, and remember to exaggerate your efforts.

8. Incorporate the signs into other parts of your daily routine. Whenever you say PLEASE or THANK YOU, make the sign. Add YOU'RE WELCOME whenever appropriate. Remember that your child needs to see other signing situations and applications to fully grasp how Good Manners signs should be used and in what circumstances.

9. SORRY is another sign that can be used throughout the day. Introduce it when there's a logical opportunity to do so.

10. Reinforce the SORRY sign with a long face and down-turned mouth to communicate your sorrow. As always, exaggerate.

11. Use SORRY when managing your child's behavior. Instruct him to tell others that he's SORRY about certain actions or behaviors and encourage him to use the sign.

12. Don't force the issue. Encourage your child to use signs but don't demand it. Example: "Joey, wouldn't you like to say you're SORRY to Sarah? Maybe you'd like to show Sarah the sign, too?"

13. When your child responds by making the SORRY (or any) sign, give him lots of praise. As we said earlier, pleasing you is the primary motivation for making these signs in the first place. Example: "Amanda, you made the sign perfectly! Keep up the good work!"

Behind the Signs

In one of my early workshops, a mother wanted her daughter to learn the signs in the Good Manners category before any others. There was just no way that she was going to raise an impolite child, she told me. I suggested that there were other signs that she (and you) should introduce first, because they have more immediate benefit—HURT and HELP, for example. Good Manners is icing on the cake.

Behavior and Safety

DON'T TOUCH	SIT
GENTLE TOUCH	SLEEP
GOOD	SLOW
HELP	SPEAK
HOT	STOP
LISTEN	WAIT
NO	WHERE
QUIET	YES
SHARE	

The Behavior and Safety category has as many positive benefits for your child as it does for you. It allows him to exercise a sense of control over his relationships with others, promotes a better sense of self and helps him grow as an individual.

Instead of pushing, pulling, and crying, a child can simply say or sign SHARE. Rather than letting himself be bullied, a child can just sign STOP. While this may not totally solve the problem (especially if the "bully" doesn't understand sign language), your little signer will feel more empowered and his overall body language will help convey his meaning.

Parents can use these signs as a way to reinforce positive behavior and to provide safety instructions. A physical gesture adds more clout to what you're saying, plus it motivates your child to pay closer attention to you.

Tips and Techniques

1. Since your child needs to make a personal connection (or association) in order for the light bulb to turn on over his head, wait for a situation when something negative occurs. (My bet is that you won't have to wait too long.) Then deal one-on-one with the situation, using your tone of voice, facial expression, and body language to help convey your message—along with the sign.

2. The manner in which you model each sign will help get your meaning across. For example, STOP (the side of one hand coming down in a chopping motion on the palm of the other hand) should be made clearly, decisively, and emphatically, and then repeated, if necessary. It's the same thing with NO (your middle and index fingers snap to the thumb).

3. Remember to offer verbal praise to your toddler and to reinforce your approval with a sign: GOOD job! (Fingertips touch your lips and move slightly away from your mouth.)

Take Note

This is from the Be-Careful-What-You-Wish-For—Department: Don't be surprised when your toddler looks at you one day and gives you a double-whammy! Not only will he *tell* you that the answer is NO but he'll reinforce the fact that he means business by making the sign for NO at the same time. What are you going to do, wash his mouth out with soap, and his hands, too?

4. While this deviates from my normal advice, on occasion, silence can be golden. Take the following scenario: Let's say you're outdoors and you see your little Christopher on the other side of the playground. You see that he is pushing his way toward the front of the line to go down the slide. You can walk over there yourself, pull him out of the line and admonish him in front of all the other children on the playground. Or you can simply call, "Christopher!" and with a disapproving look on your face, sign STOP or NO.

5. Introduce the other signs when it seems logical. Since signs need to be taught in context, wait for a relevant situation. In other words, wait for a situation when you would naturally say the *word*, then add its sign.

6. While the rationale behind most other signs is obvious, I need to make a few comments about several of them:

   ◆ GENTLE TOUCH. This is a good sign to teach when a friend brings her infant to visit. Just as you use a stern voice for STOP, now your tone becomes calm and soothing. It's also a good sign to use when there is a new pet in the family. Many children like to grab or squeeze pets and need to be encouraged to take a more gentle approach.

   ◆ DON'T TOUCH. This is a combination of the NO and TOUCH signs. I'll bet it will become one of your most popular signs.

   ◆ HELP. This is a wonderful sign to teach your child. Not only does it reduce frustration (especially if a child is not speaking yet) but also shows him that assistance is only a sign away.

It will help if you become proactive in this area. Be on the lookout for a time when your child needs some kind of assistance and before he can become agitated or frustrated, come to his rescue with "Bobby, do you need HELP?"

Note: The HELP sign is shown in two versions in our dictionary. Help #1 has been adapted from ASL to make it easier for a toddler to produce. Which one you use is up to you.

Games and Activities

BALL	HIDE
BOOK	JUMP
DANCE	MINE
FALL	MUSIC

PLAY	WALK
RUN	WASH
SLEEP	YOURS

By the time your child is a toddler, you really don't have to worry about bombarding him with too much information—or too many signs. Children's brains have an amazing ability to take in an incredible amount of information and sort it all out. It's like teaching words. You say a certain word over and over, emphasizing it as much as possible. When a child is ready and able to repeat it back to you, he will.

Tips and Techniques

1. The signs in this category will serve as an additional method and motivation for your child to express himself while adding to his signing vocabulary. Since most of these signs look like what they represent (iconic), they will be easy for your child and you to remember.

2. A brief demonstration is all you need to introduce the more obvious signs. The first time you read a book, show the sign for BOOK. "See how I can make my hands open like a BOOK? That's the way we make the sign!"

3. The same goes for BALL. "I'm going to make a sign and I bet you can guess what I'm signing. Yes, it's a BALL! Can you try?"

4. Promote the use of signs by asking your child to choose. "Do you want to play BALL or read a BOOK? Can you speak and sign your choice?"

5. Introduce MUSIC and DANCE together for their obvious correlation.

6. Sign PLAY and RUN as part of your routine. Maintain a signing dialog. "Would you like to PLAY? Let's see how fast you can RUN?"

7. When it's time for naptime or rest, make the sign for SLEEP and maintain its ongoing use.

8. When it's time to WASH after an activity or before snack time, make the sign and incorporate it into your routine. Keep encouraging your toddler to use it as you do.

9. Use books to teach the signs. Point to a picture, say the word and demonstrate the sign. Ask your child to do the same.

10. Again, when it's appropriate for you to use a word and you know the sign, go for it.

Feelings and Emotions

ANGRY	HOT
COLD	HUG
CRY	HURT
FRIGHTENED	LOVE
FUNNY	SAD
HAPPY	

The benefits of encouraging your toddler to express his emotions by using words and related signs are obvious. When you do so, it validates his right to feel the way he is feeling. Plus it gives him a way to let people know exactly how he feels, especially if he isn't able to articulate it. Simply put, signing reduces the alternatives: whining, crying, and kicking, to name just a few.

Tips and Techniques

1. As you're already doing, no doubt, continue to let your toddler know that having a certain feeling or reaction is fine—but that expressing that emotion by talking about it, and signing it, is even better.

2. Use books where characters convey specific emotions. Ask questions that promote a discussion of emotions and their related signs. "How do you think the three bears felt when they saw that Goldilocks ate their porridge? Do you think they were ANGRY? Have you ever been ANGRY?"

3. Consider creative role-playing to promote the use and understanding of different emotions and signs. Use body language and exaggerated facial expressions to better communicate the meaning of the signs. Play it up. Have fun!

4. While it isn't a true feeling or emotion, I have included the sign for HURT in this category since it's something that can result in crying or emotional upheaval. HURT is a very important sign for you to know and teach. Since it's a bit more complex than some of the other signs, newcomers to the program should read more about how to introduce and reinforce the sign in Chapter 4.

Animals

ALLIGATOR	GIRAFFE
BEAR	HORSE
CAT	KANGAROO
COW	LION
DOG	MONKEY
ELEPHANT	RABBIT
FISH	SNAKE
FROG	

Sometimes in our endeavor to promote the use of signing to toddlers, we lose sight of the fact that it can be just plain fun! No, it isn't necessary that your child know the animal signs, but he will enjoy learning them—and you will, too.

Tips and Techniques

1. Introduce the signs for the various animals in a lesson devoted to the topic.

2. Model the sign for each animal using an animal picture-book.

3 Reinforce the sign and the name of the animal by asking your child to sign and make the noise the animal makes.

4. Have your toddler make the sign and have others guess what the animal is.

5. Take your child to the zoo so he can show off what he has learned and see the "genuine articles" firsthand.

6. It doesn't matter what or how many animal signs you teach. Teach them just for the joy of it.

Smart Signs

One of the best ways to reinforce signs is to make them interactive experiences for your child. When teaching your child animal signs, for example, a trip to the zoo takes on a whole new dimension. Not only will he see his picture-book animals come alive, but he'll have something to talk about for days. If he knows the signs, that is.

Toilet Training

DIAPER CHANGE   FINISHED/ALL DONE

POTTY/TOILET

The age of your child obviously affects your goal in this area. If your toddler is still in diapers, then showing the DIAPER CHANGE sign when changing him would be in your best interest. By the way, if you haven't already done so, Chapter 4 will help you introduce that sign.

Your primary focus here is toilet or potty training. It goes without saying that these suggestions should be adapted according to the age of your own toddler.

Tips and Techniques

1. Decide on one word—POTTY or TOILET—and stick with it. (I will use POTTY. Both signs are the same.)

2. Keep to your current toilet training strategy, adding the sign wherever applicable.

3. Encourage other caregivers to use the sign consistently with your child.

4. Pay attention to the clues that your toddler may give that he needs to use the potty. Then ask him verbally and by signing if he needs to use the POTTY.

5. As with anything else, praise always works when a child uses a sign. "Good for you. You remembered the sign for POTTY!"

6. Use children's books that focus on potty training to introduce and reinforce the sign.

7. While saying the word is always encouraged, showing the sign to an older toddler who looks like he may need to use the toilet may serve as a nonembarrassing reminder for your child when he's in a group with others.

There you have it! We are FINISHED/ALL DONE! You now know all there is to know about teaching your baby or toddler to sign. When you think about it, it's all very easy, don't you agree? The trick is to make it as natural and as enjoyable as possible.

Speaking of enjoyable, I had a wonderful time sharing my signing know-how with you. And I would love to know how you are doing. Remember, if you need HELP, I'm just an e-mail address away at diane@kindersigns.com.

Good luck and happy signing!

The Least You Need to Know

◆ There are no right or wrong ways to introduce signs to your toddler.

◆ When you learn a sign language principle or technique, it can generally be applied to all signing categories.

◆ The best way to teach any sign in any category is to make it personal and relevant.

◆ Select signs and categories that are of interest to you and your child.

◆ Don't worry about bombarding your toddler with too many signs. With repetition and reinforcement, he'll sort it all out.

Appendix A

Questions I'm Asked the Most

What's on Everyone's Mind?

Will sign language interfere with my baby's speech and language development?

On the contrary! Research has proven conclusively that babies who sign speak *earlier* and have larger vocabularies than babies who don't sign. Simply put, sign language will accelerate your baby's language development, not hinder it.

What will my baby be able to "tell" me?

Your baby can communicate when he's hungry, thirsty, or wants you to read another book to him. He can even let you know when he has an earache or needs a diaper change. It all depends on what signs you teach him.

When should I begin teaching sign language to my baby?

As a general rule, around six or seven months, but it's different for each baby. To determine if your baby is ready to begin, look for signs that your baby has enough long-term memory to re-member the signs and the manual dexterity to imitate them.

How fast will my baby "catch on" to signing?

Again, each baby is different. In general, if you start when your baby is around six or seven months, you will see results eight to ten weeks later. It depends on your baby's age and how often and consistent your signing efforts are. The older your baby, the faster he will catch on. Babies who are 12 months or older may associate signs and their meanings in a matter of days.

When will my baby stop signing?

Most babies will stop signing when they find out that spoken words are more effective that gesturing. But some may keep a few signs to emphasize a point or to help them when they're not being understood. Again, it all depends on the baby.

What's the most important benefit of signing with my baby?

In my opinion, it's reduced frustration. When your baby is able to tell you what he wants or needs, he has little or no need to be frustrated. Life becomes less stressful for everyone.

How many signs will I have to learn?

That's up to you. We include over 100 signs in this program and have categorized them according to use. While there are some basic signs that we recommend, after that it's up to you and your baby.

Do you use American Sign Language (ASL)?

Yes, our program is based on American Sign Language (ASL), the official language of the deaf community in the United States. It's a great way to start your baby on the road to being bilingual.

Can sign language of another country be substituted?

People from other countries have written to me to tell me that they have successfully used British Sign Language (BSL) and Irish Sign Language (ISL) with the program. It doesn't matter which sign language you use. Just follow the guidelines in our program and substitute your sign language of choice.

My baby is in daycare. How will that affect his signing?

More and more daycare centers are using sign language to communicate with the babies in their care. Among other benefits, childcare professionals have discovered that there's less crying in a facility where babies sign. But even if your daycare provider doesn't offer signing expertise, you can still experience signing success at home. It may just take you a little longer. An even better idea? Try to convince your provider to get with the program!

My baby is over two years. Will he benefit from sign language?

A baby's brain is primed for maximum language development until the age of three. Plus, signing gives toddlers an outlet for expressing themselves when they can't come up with the words they need. So, the answer is a resounding, Yes!

Is it true that signing eliminates the "terrible twos"?

While signing may not *eliminate* the "terrible twos," it can make the stage more bearable! Since toddlers understand more than they can verbally express at this stage, they often become frustrated. The result is a wide range of negative behaviors, including temper tantrums. Sign language gives toddlers a viable outlet to express themselves.

We speak two languages in our home. Should we sign to our daughter in both languages?

What a wonderful opportunity for your baby! Make sure he hears and learns both languages. To make it easier in the early years, I suggest that one parent speaks and signs in English and the other communicates only with speech in the second language.

I have adopted a three-year-old little girl from Russia who speaks no English. Should I sign with her?

While signing won't hurt her and may even help reduce her frustration level, many parents in similar situations get too wrapped up in signing when the primary goal is to teach the child English. If you feel you can use signs as part of a support system, one that complements your verbal language efforts, then I suggest that you give it a try. But if you are nervous or unsure about it, then focus on verbal language alone.

I can't seem to understand what my baby girl is signing. What should I do?

It depends on the situation. Trying looking for additional clues from her. What is she looking at when she's making a certain sign? What about her body language? That might also help you decipher what she wants. If you still can't figure it out, relax. It'll eventually click.

How do I motivate my baby to sign?

Try gently shaping his hands to make a certain sign or tapping them to give your baby the idea that you want him to use his hands to communicate. Just remember not to use or express disappointment when it doesn't happen. Your baby will sign when he's ready.

My baby is getting her signs mixed up. How do I correct her?

You correct her with repetition and by example. It's the same way you would correct her if she said a word incorrectly. If she is making the sign for "shoes" when she means "socks," get out her shoes and sign and say "shoes." Do the same with socks. Do it a few times and she'll see the error of her ways!

My baby was making progress and now nothing is happening. What happened to his signs?

Maybe he has other things on his mind, like teething or learning to walk. Sometimes babies just take a signing "hiatus." The important thing to remember is for you to stay on track. Keep signing as before. Chances are, he'll be back.

How do I convince my husband and other family members that this works?

Give them this book and highlight the research. But if that doesn't work, go it alone! It's too important an opportunity to pass up. My guess is that once the naysayers see how much fun you're having and how positively your baby is responding, they'll eventually join you in the effort.

Fun and Games

Activities to Encourage Your Baby to Sign

While signing should become part of your daily routine, activities and games that include the signs your baby already knows are an additional source of enjoyment for him. Plus they'll serve as an effective reinforcement tool.

Baby Concentration

Cut out pictures of favorite and familiar objects. Make a copy of each one. Turn them over and play "concentration." This game is an ideal way to reinforce signs when you use pictures of signing objects (BALL, BOOK, etc.). Even if your baby can't discover the "pairs," do it for him, *talking* every step of the way as you select one object (sign) and then find its match.

Animal Cover-Up

Get out a favorite animal book and place a paper over a certain animal. Then sign the animal's name. For example, ask and sign,

"WHERE is the LION?" Uncover the lion's picture and celebrate your "discovery," saying and signing, "There's the LION!"

Hide and Seek

Use the sign for WHERE with objects that you hide. "WHERE is the BOOK?" or "WHERE is the SHOE?" Then watch your baby's amazement as you make the object magically appear! When he's old enough, let him look for and find the object himself.

Here's another variation: Let your baby see you hide a BALL under a blanket and let him search for it (or you find it for him). Increase his attention span and signing vocabulary by hiding two or three objects at once.

Photo Album

Nothing works better than getting out the old photo album to teach signs for family members. Take your baby's finger gently and point to each member of the family while you make the sign and say the word. Make sure to point out his own picture to learn the sign BABY.

The Walking Tour

Take a walk around your house and "introduce" your baby to everyone and everything he meets. Stress the name of each object and if you know it, add the sign.

The Good Night Tour

Make it a routine to sign and say goodnight to everyone and everything on the route to bed. After the family members, say good night to the dog, cat, even the telephone. Silly? You bet. But it's another opportunity to reinforce the signs you want your baby to learn.

Field Trips

A walk in the park, a trip to the zoo, an hour in the back yard. They're all educational signing adventures to your little one.

Grab Bag

Fill a laundry sack with signing objects like BOOK, BALL, TEDDY BEAR, etc. Then without looking, reach in the bag and pull out one of them. Make a show of it and act surprised when something comes out of the bag. Then sign and say the word.

Use Stand-Ins

While your baby is watching, "ask" his doll or Teddy if he'd like something to EAT or DRINK. Maybe he'd prefer MILK. Maybe poor Teddy bumped his head and is in PAIN. You get the idea.

Sing and Sign

Sing and sign to Itsy-Bitsy-Spider, Old Mac Donald, and any other song you can think of. Or take a familiar melody and make up your own lyrics that include your targeted signs.

Read Books

Read as much as you can with your baby, adding signs as you go. Babies love repetition, so make sure you read the same book over and over.

Activities and Ideas to Stimulate Your Baby's Brain

Do whatever you can to provide new and varied opportunities and experiences for your baby. Every sight, touch, and smell stimulates his growing brain.

Play Imitation Games

When your baby is very little, imitate his babbling and facial expressions. As he gets older, play simple variations of "Simon Says."

Change His Outlook

Give your baby an occasional new outlook on life by varying the position of his crib or moving the position of his high chair.

Use Overhead Toys and Mobiles

Make sure there's always something available to intrigue and visually interest your baby.

Make a Foggy Face

Hold your baby up to a fogged mirror. As you wipe sections clean, talk about what you see as your baby's face magically appears.

Play Peek-A-Boo

This simple activity will stimulate your baby's brain, especially when you add some surprise variations.

Problem Solve

Hide a favorite object under a blanket, pillow, or in your pocket. Exaggerate your efforts until you find it. Let your baby or toddler participate in this problem-solving activity as he gets older.

Play Take-a-Way

Place three familiar objects on the floor and talk about each one. Then put a blanket over them while "secretly" removing one. Then remove the blanket and talk about the objects that are there and see if your baby looks for the one that's missing. As he gets older, increase the number of objects in the game.

Play Sequencing Games

Encourage your baby to imitate different clapping sequences and rhythms. Hold his hands and clap for him if he's not old enough. Or use colored blocks or colored cereal pieces as part of a sequencing activity. Say the colors out loud, "Blue, yellow, green. What comes next?" Then recreate the pattern. Make it a do-it-yourself game until your baby is old enough to participate himself.

Smell and Touch

Let your baby smell the differences between sweet and sour. Then let him feel something silky on his hand compared to something rough like sand paper or a scrub brush.

Talk to Your Baby

Speak in sentences, have conversations, ask and answer your own questions if you have to—but make sure that your baby is bombarded with the sounds and rhythms of language.

Play Music

Play classical music around the house. It's a wonderful way to stimulate your baby's brain and class up your own act!

Play Comparisons

Line up things that are of the same category but different sizes. Three shoes, three plates etc. Then put them in size order, saying "big, bigger, biggest." Mix them up and do it again.

Sign with Your Baby

I couldn't leave that out, now could I?

Appendix C

Resources

Online Resources

The Internet offers a wealth of information on sign language and early childhood education. The following have been selected as great places for additional research and valuable resources to make signing with your baby easier and more enjoyable.

American Sign Language (ASL) Dictionaries

ASL Sign Language Browser (http://commtechlab.msu.edu/sites/aslweb/browser.htm). An extensive sign language dictionary of animated signs from the Communications Technology Lab at Michigan State University. A great complement to the Baby Sign Language Dictionary in this book.

ASL Pro (www.aslpro.com). An online American Sign Language dictionary that offers more than 6,000 useful signs.

Continued Instruction in American Sign Language

ASL University (www.lifeprint.com). A free resource for American Sign Language students, instructors, interpreters, and parents of deaf children. Hearing children may also benefit.

Signing Online (www.signingonline.com). Fee-based programs that provide the basics you need to become fluent in American Sign Language.

Speech and Language Disorders

The American Speech-Language-Hearing Association (ASHA) (www.asha.org). The professional association for speech-language pathologists and audiologists. Research information on speech and language disorders and delays.

Speech Delay (www.speechdelay.com). A resource for parents and caregivers dealing with speech and language delayed children.

Down Syndrome Directory (www.downsyndrome.com). A directory of Down Syndrome organizations and comprehensive websites on the topic.

Early Childhood Education and Development

Zero to Three/Brainwonders (www.zerotothree.org/brainwonders/). A comprehensive and interactive resource for parents and early childhood education professionals on healthy development of children from birth to age three.

Healthy Start—U.S. Dept. of Education (www.ed.gov/parents/early-child/ready/healthystart/index.html). Twelve booklets, each focused on one month in a baby's life. An initiative of Laura Bush when she was First Lady of Texas; now revised and distributed by the U.S. Department of Agriculture, U.S. Department of Education, and U.S. Department of Health and Human Services.

Baby Sign Language Forums

KinderSigns Support Group (http://kinderworkshops.com/ bbparents). Connect with other families and get signing ideas from other parents at the KinderSigns support group.

Parents and Educators at Berkeley (http://parents.berkeley.edu/ advice/babies/signing.html). Share your sign language experiences with a California-based group of parents and professionals.

Sign with Your Baby **Online Forum (http://groups.yahoo.com/ group/signwithyourbaby/).** Find parents and supporters of Joseph Garcia's *Sign with Your Baby* program.

Baby Sign Language Instructor Training

Baby Sign Language Instructors (www.kindersigns.com/bizopps. htm). An opportunity to learn more about joining the KinderSigns network of instructors and teach baby sign language in your own community.

Baby Sign Language Training for Childcare Professionals

www.kindersigns.com/www/Baby-Childcare-Edition.htm. Information and instruction for childcare providers on how to enhance their curriculum with sign language for babies and toddlers.

Books for Your Baby

Bang, Molly. *Ten, Nine, Eight.* Greenwillow, 1996.

Brown, Marc. *Play Rhymes.* Puffin, reprint edition, 1993.

Brown, Margaret Wise. *Goodnight Moon.* Harper Festival, board edition, 1991.

Freeman, Don. *Corduroy.* Viking Juvenile, 1968.

Glazer, Tom. *Eye Winker, Tom Tinker Chin Chopper: 50 Musical Finger Plays.* Doubleday Books for Young Readers, reissue edition, 1978.

Hill, Eric. *Where's Spot?* Putnam Publishing Group, board edition, 2003.

Joosse, Barbara. *Mama, Do You Love Me?* Chronicle Books, board edition, 1998.

Keats, Ezra Jack. *Peter's Chair.* Puffin Books, reprint edition, 1998.

Layton, Meredith. *Baby's First Words* (Sign & Say Interactive Language Series). Peek-A-Boo Publishing, 1999.

Marzollo, Jean. *I Spy Little Animals.* Cartwheel, board edition, 1998.

Miller, Margaret. *Baby Faces.* Little Simon, board edition, 1998.

———. *Peekaboo Baby.* Little Simon, board edition, 2001.

Opie, Iona (editor). *My First Mother Goose.* Candlewick, first U.S. edition, 1996.

Oxenbury, Helen. *Clap Hands.* Little Simon, board edition, 1999.

Prelutsky, Jack. *Read Aloud Rhymes for the Very Young.* Knopf Books for Young Readers, reissue edition, 1986.

Tafuri, Nancy. *Have You Seen My Duckling?* Harper Trophy, reprint edition, 1991.

Touch and Feel: Home by Dorling Kindersley Publishing, DK Children, board edition, 1998.

Touch and Feel: Farm by Dorling Kindersley Publishing, DK Children, board edition, 1998.

Touch and Feel: Wild Animals by Dorling Kindersley Publishing, DK Children, first edition, 1998.

Williams, Vera. *"More, More, More" Said the Baby.* Greenwillow, board edition, 1997.

Books for You

Acredolo, Linda, and Susan Goodwyn. *Baby Signs: How To Talk with Your Baby Before Your Baby Can Talk.* Contemporary Books (a division of the McGraw-Hill Companies), 2002.

———. *Baby Minds: Brain Building Games Your Baby Will Love.* Bantam Books, 2000.

Daniels, Marilyn. *Dancing with Words: Signing for Hearing Children's Literacy.* Bergin & Garvey, 2001.

Garcia, Joseph. *Sign with Your Baby: How to Communicate with Infants Before They Can Speak.* Stratton-Kehl Publications, Inc., 2000.

Baby Sign Language Journal

Keep track of your baby's signing progress by entering the date that you introduce a sign and the date when your baby masters it. Keep a copy on your refrigerator so babysitters or other caregivers can communicate with your baby when you're not at home.

More

Bring your fingertips together a few times.

Introduced: _____

Mastered: _____

Notes: _____
_____
_____
_____
_____
_____

Eat

Your hand moves back and forth to your mouth as if eating.

Introduced: _____

Mastered: _____

Notes: _____

_____

_____

_____

_____

Milk

Your hand opens and closes as if you're milking a cow.

Introduced: _____

Mastered: _____

Notes: _____

_____

_____

_____

_____

Hurt/Pain

The tips of your index fingers touch.

Introduced: _____

Mastered: _____

Notes: _____

_____

_____

_____

_____

Help

Your palms are flat and tap your chest twice. (Adapted from ASL.)

Introduced: _____

Mastered: _____

Notes: _____

_____

_____

_____

_____

Diaper Change

All fingers except your thumb fold to your palms. Bring your knuckles together and pivot in opposite directions.

Introduced: _____

Mastered: _____

Notes: _____

_____

_____

_____

_____

Bottle

Pretend to grip a bottle with one hand and place it on the palm of your other hand.

Introduced: _____

Mastered: _____

Notes: _____

_____

_____

_____

_____

Drink

Pretend you are holding a glass and taking a sip.

Introduced: _____

Mastered: _____

Notes: _____

_____

_____

_____

_____

_____

Finished/All Done

Both palms face upward and then turn over and outward.

Introduced: _____

Mastered: _____

Notes: _____

_____

_____

_____

_____

_____

Water

Make a "W" with three fingers and place them at the corner of your mouth.

Introduced: _____

Mastered: _____

Notes: _____

_____

_____

_____

_____

Down

Your index finger points downward.

Introduced: _____

Mastered: _____

Notes: _____

_____

_____

_____

_____

Up

Your index finger points upward.

Introduced: _____

Mastered: _____

Notes: _____

_____

_____

_____

_____

_____

Use the following space to jot down notes to caregivers, progress made on specific signs, etc.

Index

Check Out These
Best-Sellers

Read by millions!

Grammar and Style
SECOND EDITION

Laurie E. Rozakis, Ph.D.

1-59257-115-8
$16.95

Buying and Selling a Home
FOURTH EDITION

Shelley O'Hara and Nancy D. Lewis

1-59257-120-4
$18.95

Being a Groom
SECOND EDITION

Jennifer Lata Rung and Mark Rung

0-02-864456-5
$9.95

Learning Spanish
THIRD EDITION

Gail Stein

0-02-864451-4
$18.95

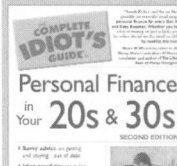

Personal Finance in Your 20s & 30s
SECOND EDITION

Sarah Young Fisher and Susan Shelly

0-02-864374-7
$19.95

Organizing Your Life
FOURTH EDITION

Georgene Lockwood

1-59257-413-0
$16.95

Total Nutrition
FOURTH EDITION

Joy Bauer, M.S., R.D., C.D.N.

1-59257-439-4
$18.95

Positive Dog Training

Pamela Dennison

0-02-864463-8
$14.95

The Bible
THIRD EDITION

James Stuart Bell and Stan Campbell

1-59257-389-4
$18.95

Calculus

W. Michael Kelley

0-02-864365-8
$18.95

Music Theory
SECOND EDITION

Michael Miller

1-59257-437-8
$19.95

The Perfect Resume
THIRD EDITION

Susan Ireland

0-02-864440-9
$14.95

Playing the Guitar
SECOND EDITION

Frederick Noad

0-02-864244-9
$21.95

Manga

John Layman and Hetti Hubler

1-59257-335-5
$19.95

Knitting and Crocheting
SECOND EDITION
Illustrated

Barbara Breiter and Gail Diven

1-59257-089-5
$16.95

More than 450 titles available at booksellers and online retailers everywhere

ALPHA